Dear Wallace

MEANDERINGS OF A
SENIOR SOLO TRAVELER

D.L. DICKSON

DEAR WALLACE

Meanderings of a Senior Solo Traveler

Copyright © 2023 by D.L. Dickson

Book formatting by Saqib_arshad

Printed in the United States of America

Dedication – to Dreamers

To my mother, Lilyan, who had wanderlust in the years when women did not have many choices, so she traveled in her retirement years – sans job … sans husband …sans children.

To the generations that followed her - to women of all ages who want to travel, and dare do so on their own, especially senior travelers, go before it's too late.

Dust off those youthful dreams.

Meander to the mountains, rivers, oceans, cities of your state or across your country's borders to another culture with another language - a new adventure.

Muster up your courage and go.

And those of you who are lucky enough to count youth on your side, have no regrets but rather memories in your 'aged' years.

Laila + Cynthia
Enjoy your
meandering - go
again - Toujours Paris -
Diane

CONTENTS

Paris is Always a Good Idea: Now & Yesterday

"We travel for years without much idea of what we are seeking. We wander in the tumult, entangled in desires and regrets. Then suddenly we arrive at one of those two or three places which are waiting for each of us patiently in this world."

- ALBERT CAMUS

Have I been reading Albert Camus lately? No. But Paris waited for me at 18, and it still waits for me 50 years later.

Why go when youth is gone, and confidence has waned?

Might you and I be part of the same conversation? In a store or at the doctor's, words like' hon',' sweetie', 'dear' are creeping in just like 'Right here in River City'. You realize they are referring to you- not your mother. You might as well be invisible like wallpaper which barely exists now, but in reality, it is coming back. We can too. We can be the comeback kids.

The truth is you still feel a bit radical, rebellious in these times, yet your voice seems diminished. "What do I do now? Is this all there is?' you say. "I wanted to see the world – What happened?" You got married, devoted your life to your kids/ husband and/or you finished school, got a job, climbed the corporate ladder. Now forty or fifty years later, you missed your backpacking opportunity to see Europe.

You think you're too old - too afraid – too set in your ways? Just go for it . What do you have to lose? Do you care what others think? Expand

1

your circle – throw a pebble out into still water and see the rings it makes. Put on your sneakers or orthopedic shoes. Let one step lead you on the journey you never took. Your mantra: "I am woman. Hear me Roar."

Fifty years later, my younger self told me to go to Paris, the place of my dreams, and stay for more than a few days. I took her advice and booked an apartment in Paris for a month. Come along on my journey at age 68.

They say age considers, youth ventures. That may be, but I was determined to take a leap of faith, and not be that woman – the one who waits by her phone for the call to set the day's agenda or to be in the group of women at a restaurant who deal with the bill as though it is the national debt. Don't mean to criticize, but you know in your heart how we can't divide up the bill for a meal. There are those that assume just dividing by the number at the table is fair despite that they are the ones who ordered the most expensive meal, three glasses of wine, dessert, and coffee. Then there are those who whip out the calculator – not the one on their cell but the one from 1986 they keep in their purse. 'The let's divide the bill equally' are the same ones who refuse to leave a decent tip even though they have asked for substitutions that don't exist and for separate checks after the waitress has presented the bill in total.

I needed to leave that nest of hens and the all-consuming food interest to follow the advice of a wise woman: "A woman over forty should make up her mind not her face." No longer a 'Leslie Caron' Gigi or a 'Gigi Hadid' gamine and well over forty, I was determined to venture and concentrate on making up my mind and not over do the face. With my personal landscape clear of children, home, and job the question of "Why not Paris?" keeps popping up. After all, the French appreciate "une femme d'un certain age". Not the coarse equivalent of our American 'cougar', but rather that vast expanse of age between a bikini clad stilettoed Brigitte Bardot from St Tropez and a leopard house coated 'Golden Girl' with mule slippers from Miami. Since I am more than halfway between one and the other, I decided it was time to break away.

Not content to binge on Grace and Frankie and Hallmark movies in my robe or go to my grandchildren's endless ballgames in my stylish black 'slimming' leggings, I needed to hit my own homeruns before it was too late. No friends could or would make that leap of faith, and since I was getting closer to the leopard lady by the minute, I went alone.

I pulled up the anchors of suburbia and found that I had no compass. I was set to head out to sea without provisions, nets, or goals. In childhood we are told to follow our dreams, but when those dreams have been met – what then? There are no more ribbons or trophies and no more races to be won. The graduations and the degrees have been accomplished. The jobs are done, the money earned, the houses bought… "What is left"?

I needed to find out. From Oprah's advice to today's 'mindfulness' we are told to live in the present, to enjoy, and to savor the moment. But when you have been on the treadmill all your life, it's hard to get off. However, that is not an excuse to sit in your robe and devour chocolate and eat ice cream out of the container. Just because we grow up and grow old, we should not stop dreaming. In reality, we have just forgotten where we put our dreams: in our son's baseball bag, our daughter's swim locker, behind our mother's chair, or in our office file cabinet under 'tomorrow'/ 'someday'.

I was so busy providing and doing for others - my dreams took a back seat. I was busy working to support my children. I had not taken the time to recalibrate my dreams, but one must make the time. Our dreams are the road maps for our hearts.

In youth we live in each moment and have no expectations or concept of time. Then we change. We no longer hear the drops of rain on rooftops and windowpanes, see the rays of sunlight that dance across the floor or notice the first crocuses peeking through the snow, or feel a sweet kiss and the softness of skin on skin. Life's enchanting song becomes replaced by rigidity, necessity, even apathy. Age and responsibilities erode our 'joie de vivre'.

I decided to step aside and go back in time – a time with no great expectations and schedules. On the pathway to new dreams, I intend to fill the 'now' time of my own inner clock with joyous pieces of moments like slivers of chocolate and bubbles of champagne.

What better than to walk through that little piece of earth called PARIS. Whether in my teens or in my sixties, I've always wanted to live in Paris. My first trip at eighteen set the course.

To fearlessly venture out on my own at 18 was never a thought, but at 60 plus? Friends said, 'what about terrorists, pickpockets, and even the 'French'. *The French* – said as though their disapproval of McDonald's makes them the enemy. My friends' words did set negative thoughts in motion. I thought maybe it wasn't such a good idea. But then the light bulb went off - why not? As a product of the Cold War, Vietnam, the civil rights movement and the assassination of JFK, I felt my times/my roads were from the start absurdly set on the blade of a knife and nothing protected or predicted what I and my generation would face over the next 50 years.

Life cannot be redone or placed on pause. Thomas Wolfe said, "There is only one voyage, the first, the last, the only one." I agreed so I took off for an idyllic journey, possibly an adventure, and at the very least- a birthday month in Paris. Not April in Paris but rather September after the tourists leave and the 'rentree' (return of children to school) begins. Women of all ages, not just pack packing girls on a gap year can travel alone. We do not have to be hamsters on the 'tour' wheel.

We can plan a journey and step into the unknown and live again. For those who were in Paris when they were young and for those who wish they had been, Paris is never too late. Paris will still be a part of you for as long as you live. Take a weekend, a week, a month, a year and breathe in the air of Paris. It has always had a certain smell to me – not the scent of lavender fields forever nor the odor of gas, trash, and ethnic food of New York. Whether 18 or 68 as soon as I open the taxi, bus, or metro doors I smell the familiar smell of adventure, of dreams, of happiness... of Paris.

I plan to have a birthday lunch at Cafe des Deux Moulins, the café in the movie Amelie, and walk the hills of Montmartre from the great stairs at the bottom of the Butte to the street up to Sacre Coeur and maybe see a lone saxophone player playing riffs of Jazz on that sidewalk overlooking all of Paris. I will be 68 on one of those last days of September – Indian summer days my mother used to call them. Such was a day when I was born. This year will be the same, Paris promises such.

Ladies, Paris is a city of possibilities. The Paris of my imagination was formed by those old movies – "Gigi', "An American in Paris, "Funny Face". They colored my youthful dreams of dancing along the banks of the Seine, dining in chandeliered ballroom with dinner courses on Sevres or Limoges China or sipping coffee at bistro tables with black and white straw backed chairs, and of shopping in designer stores with hatboxes and pristine logo shopping bags tangling from my arm. Meeting the tall dark handsome Frenchman was high on my list. Few of those things happened, but I still can experience the flush of youth when I think about them and have memories of the things that really happened. Hope springs eternal and planning my trip, I anticipate the best possible Paris.

I am an independent woman not a woman of independent means. This translates to I take care of myself by myself. I am not independently wealthy, not living off of papa's inheritance or an ex's fat divorce settlement but from a teacher's pension. "The Road not Taken..." does not apply to me. I chose the trodden down one – the commonsense one – the road most people take. I had to work for a living. I felt I could not slide off the path since there was no one to pick me up and put me back on. I never felt I could 'drop out'. My mother could not foot the bill for my mistakes. No bra burning for me. No lace or pastel -colored ones to wear, just practical white ones from Sears Roebuck.

College was a privilege not a given. Scholarships did not allow for screwing up, but it did allow for dreaming and planning.

TURNING BACK THE CLOCK

Let's step back to 1965, a decade of prim little hats and cutoff jeans... not worn together. That year was my first trip to Paris. Since then - so much has changed, yet at times I still feel like that young girl until I glance in the mirror and see my mother looking back.

I did not tell my mother what I was planning until everything was set. <u>Frommer's Europe on $5 a Day</u> became the roadmap for my journey. Beginning in high school I saved all my babysitting and lunch money. My friend Ginger and I had told our mothers we'd be going first to London to see if we could meet the Beatles then to Paris to meet a young Louis Jourdan or a leather clad Jean-Paul Belmondo. I don't remember any confrontation or hysterics. Of course, I really did not tell mom about Paul, George, Ringo, John, and Jean-Paul. The moms just assumed we had it under control. We were responsible not crazy teenagers and had a modem of commonsense.

Everything was simpler and easier back then, but maybe everything is easier when you're young. Your life does not hold a lot of comparison. I was happy with my white Keds, and my skirts and dresses made from Simplicity patterns. No, LBD- in fact, I did not even know what a little black dress was or that every chic Parisian wore black and only black. A large black patent leather gold clasped purse from Macy's in New York City and a French Twist a la Bardot comprised my 'street style'. Good enough I thought, despite the lack of a LBD. It was August, and <u>Europe on $5 a Day</u> did not buy high fashion, an air-conditioned hotel, or sumptuous meals. Bread, cheese, wine, cheap hotels, and picnicking in parks is what it bought.

On our first day in Paris, Ginger and I took a walk down the Champs-Elysees, the most beautiful and desirable avenue in the world. Before setting out from our hotel, the desk clerk told us Parisians go on vacation in August - in fact, he said all of France did.

Even as the sidewalk heat came up through the soles of my Keds, I expected to see a rush of traffic as in the black and white film 'Breathless'. Could I catch a glimpse of Jean-Paul Belmondo out of the corner of my eye? Despite the clerk's comment about the August exodus, I thought it more than strange that the Champs-Elysees was empty. In fact, we were the only two people on the Avenue. Across the street a man came running. No Belmondo, but rather a frantic gendarme, sprinted up from a metro stop. "Mesmoiselles, mesmoiselles... suivez-moi."

Not even a "s'il vous plait" as he waved his arms like a windmill to follow him – down the metro steps, through an underground passage and out to the other side.

"But we are 'Americaines'." That was our clueless explanation. I am certain he already had figured that out by our dress, walk, and accent. In addition, he knew Parisians had the good sense to leave the city in August.

He said nothing as he escorted us to the other side of the tall wall where hundreds of people were milling around. I looked down over the wall into La Place de la Concorde where the guillotine once stood more than one hundred and seventy-five years ago. Now a tiger tank turret twirled around. Flames shot out amid the deafening noise of fake ammunition being fired.

I had learned my World War II history from a French teacher who recounted stories of the War and Saint Mere Eglise. I had not stepped back into time, but the novel, <u>Is Paris Burning</u> had. Here I was In Paris in August almost twenty years to the date of August 25, 1944, the day Paris was liberated. A cold shiver ran down my spine.

That day and many other events in the Second World War paved the way for my interest in WWII. Too many coincidences made me have an affinity for that time period when Paris was liberated, August 25, 1944, and the days that followed freed Paris and the world from Nazi Germany. That history allowed me in this century to walk the streets of Paris and not run in fear as so many must have during those days of occupation. Now almost fifty years later I plan to find that young girl filled with curiosity and strength on the brink of life - and to rediscover her spirit within me.

No longer a teenager saving lunch money for my trip to Paris, I conceived a plan to save money for my Paris meanderings. I avoided E-Bay and Amazon; it's too easy to buy one more gadget or book. I had no coffee breaks with lattes, fat luncheons, or bargains from the mall. '*Just do it*'. Don't buy. Saving up for Paris was the goal. The thought of Paris tea salons, cafes, walks up the steps of Montmartre and strolls through the Luxembourg gardens made me not spend money.

My ideas were logical but not rigid. I would rent an apartment for a month- cook and save on food. Whatever my food would cost in the United States, I'd spend in Paris. Eat in Suburbia or eat in Paris not a hard choice for me. I am not a Julia Childs with a taste and talent for great food – nor do I have a husband to support me while I dabble in possible interests or courses, nor do I have the incredible 1950's exchange rate of dollars to francs, I am happy eating simple nutritious things not whipping up incredible entrees for lunch and dinner. Besides, my studio rental has a stove top and a microwave but no oven.

I looked at Airbnb and Home Away websites and narrowed my possible places down to price, space, and arrondissement. Paris consists of 20 sections or arrondissements. – think of New York City. You might want to live in a penthouse in Manhattan but will settle on a basement studio in Brooklyn. I would have liked to find a place in the 4th, 5th, 6th, or 7th but settled for the 11th – just a few blocks from the Marais in the 4th and its ritzy Place des Vosges.

I believe in signs. The street of my prospective Paris pad was on passage Saint Sebastien, my grandson's name. I negotiated a price for a month's stay. After googling it and checking out the metro (subway) stops close to familiar places and landmarks, I felt comfortable. I read reviews very carefully to see what people had to say. You do need to look at square footage. Online photos can make any place look expansive although it might be the size of a teacup. Also google map street views. Renters may include photos of cafes and parks that are nowhere near the residence. Better to have a small place in a great walkable area than a larger one far away from the things you want to see.

Day 1

SEPTEMBER 19

"Your comfort zone is your tombstone."

I hate to fly. I do not sleep. I listen to every noise. I imagine birds at 35,000 feet. I smell possible fumes. I look at the wings to make sure nothing is falling off. This time I try to just think of Paris; I am ready. I had memorized the building code to drop off my body bag of a suitcase before I hit the streets.

The afternoon was cloudy and cold in the Bastille neighborhood that would be my home for the next month. Noted for its infamous prison which became a symbol of the French revolution, nothing of it exists today but a gold tower thrust up into the sky, to mark the place of the prison, ripped down stone by stone on July 14, 1789 by the people of Paris.

No hot July days of revolution but cool September days of shopkeepers and children going back to work and school, I walk to get acquainted with this working-class neighborhood. I'm in no rush. I'm lucky to have the gift of a month. I was to have a year nearly 50 years ago, but a poor college choice and John F. Kennedy's assassination in November left me alone, disillusioned, damaged, and without financial resources to leave. I sucked it up and stayed. Those were the facts. The old adage of 'knowing what I know now' would have supplied me with the fortitude to go. But now is my time – 50 years later – without my youth but with character lines and

11

a plan to live without regret. To discover another Paris through the lined but clearer eyes of experience is the mission.

The 11th is not a tourist area. I pass women layered in bright colored fabric with scarves wrapped around their heads not around their necks. Dark skinned men hold cell phones in their palms and teenagers on skateboards shout in French slang as they jump the sidewalk and skirt the cars. The men regardless of the cut of their shirts, suits, or sweaters wear the emblem of Paris and perhaps most French cities – the scarf stylishly but casually draped around their necks. This area is like an American quilt – Thai, Chinese, North African, eastern European restaurants... Maybe if I am brave, I'll go in at night - but I am a woman ... d'un certain age, not a young 'throw caution' to the wind one" so for now I am content to enter a small park, a green spot in the 11th and stop to watch young children on swings and slides and old men playing Pétanque. The squeals of laughter and the squabbles of the men's gamesmanship make me realize we are all the same – different nationalities but the same reactions. I am on the outside looking in with the luxury of time. I am in no hurry.

"But with miles to go before I sleep" my New England upbringing makes me move on. Enough watching, I want to do. I walk the narrow, crowded sidewalks and dodge mothers holding their children's hands and grandmothers pushing baby carriages. An occasional French bulldog or pug walks in front of me. Even they walk with a purpose. They must know how to find their way home. I wander down one street and cross over to another. Anything that catches my interest I follow. I should be like the fat orange tabby lying redolent on a cushion of red beaded silk in a vintage clothing store window. He watches people go by, but unlike him I want to pounce on food. Hunger and fatigue have hit. I double back to the chain store supermarket. Open-air markets will have to wait. I'm hungry now- fresh eggs, fresher bread, camembert, butter, onions, mozzarella, parsley, chives, garlic and red table wine I place all in the wire basket.

A two-egg omelet, sliced cucumbers, camembert and a fresh baguette make a meal that would be all too simple for Julia. It did not look beautiful as it lay askew and malformed on the white plate, but I push it together – 'No excuses. No one will know." I hear her voice say in my ear as I sip wine. She would have approved of the buttered baguette and white wine set on the outside garden table. Granted the garden at summer's end was more brown than green but Julia would like the utter enjoyment of the simple meal facing the rooftop apartments under the Paris sky bordering these little squares of backyards. After all this was her Paris. She was hungry back then, and I am hungry now, so I pour another glass of wine and toast to our mutual love of Paris.

No romantic view of the Eiffel Tower or sunny Provence fields of sunflowers. The landscape is withered brown rose buds, stems of weeds and daisies in disintegrating flowerpots. A rusty rake, broken spade, and pruning shears are propped in a corner against the 9-foot-high stone wall that squares in this once green plot of earth. The building had been a granite factory. A few rose color slabs and a basin rest by the front door of the building now divided into apartments and one room flats such as mine. My one room has a pullout couch, a tiny kitchen, and a decent bathroom with a tub and shower set off the entrance hall inside the flat.

I hear music this afternoon- in reality, ten p.m. New York time. I sit at my bistro table looking up at the tall buildings surrounding these courtyard apartments. When I fall asleep, I will be able to see into the Paris sky over the walls – the doors are sliding glass so I can step out into Paris and this bit of seclusion. In the days that follow I wonder if anyone is looking down at me and wondering why I come out every morning and evening to look up with my mug of coffee or glass of wine.

That first afternoon the scratch of record player music drifts down from the only open window on the top floor of the stone building. "Autumn in New York" a New York voice in Paris. Sinatra serenades me

- what a wonderful welcome. He was the singer of my mother's era. He sang about New York, the city where I was born and where my mother worked as a young woman in the 1940's. I once had a conversation with my mother concerning Frank – she said she did not like him and was not one of his crazy crooner fans. I could not understand this. I adored him. I did not live in those times, but they were my times. The 1940's bring tears to my eyes. By the time I saw Sinatra he was old – probably as old as I am now. But the heart does not grow old - just wiser and unfortunately a bit harder.

I need to forget the past and live in the present. Berman and Bogart are not going to sit down next to me in a Latin Quarter jazz club and Yves Montand is not going to meet me in Saint Germain des Pres. Now a new song filters through the air. Billy Holliday's "I'll be seeing you in everything that's young and gay" echoes in my mind. I shake my head. I need to live in the moment, in the present, and not let my mind wander into a past that is not even mine.

Although I did not live in the 1940's of Sinatra and Montand, I feel connected to them rather than the 1960's. I should have lived here then, but I did not. Dreams bubble to the surface. I can almost see them, pink and lovely, rising– not yet popped by the thorns of life. I am here now. Today is my time.

Tomorrow is tomorrow, and I shall choose a quote and venture out – well rested, not in the1940's or 60's but in these days of a new century.

Day 2

SEPTEMBER 20

"Our happiest moments as tourists always seem to be when we stumble upon something while in pursuit of something else."

- LAWRENCE BLOCK

A perfect September day with clear skies – like that September 11th day more than a decade ago when planes hit the Twin Towers and the glass of those 'eyes of the world' shattered and killed so many. That day cut apart families and the world we knew. Although terrorists have attacked Paris long before 9/11, fear is in the consciousness more than ever. Today I choose to live life on my own terms. I step out on this sunny day in Paris and look up at the sky and do not think about planes imploding.

First stop - a croissant and a coffee to go. To 'emporter' which is unusual to ask for, but this is a working-class neighborhood and they have embraced coffee to go as they walk to work.

The patisserie/boulangerie is different. I see customers carrying long baguettes by holding them with a small square of paper in the middle or tucked under one's arm or upright in a cloth shopping bag. My croissant with almonds is placed in the same small square. I eat it as I walk with a bag over my shoulder. My bag contains a metro map and a large street map. One free hand holds the 'café crème' and the other the buttery flakey croissant. Specks fall on my scarf draped around my neck. I don't care. I'm not going to work. I am here to explore and have an adventure.

Up Passage Saint Sebastien and by the homeless encampment on the corner of Rue Ameliot. I pluck up my courage, hold my bag tighter and closer to my body, and walk past with assurance. Would I be afraid in New York? – yes, but this is Paris. I do not stop nor pass judgement. I just feel lucky, it is not me. As the days pass, he or she is one of the few I see every day.

I wander up Boulevard Beaumarchais and cross over to Pas du Mule, a very narrow street which served a commercial use hundreds of years ago but now the 'step of a mule' is just a cross - through to wider streets for cars going in both directions. I peer into shop windows. Some carry knives. Some are pop up shops with clothes from China or India, and others are little chocolate boutiques with pieces of tempting chocolate in their window. I drop in for one – a dark chocolate truffle with an almond on top to accompany the croissant I ate for breakfast. The sun is almost directly overhead so I have been wandering for a while looking for my destination: Place des Vosges.

I come upon another place, The Square Leopold Achille, which will become one of my favorites. It runs along Rue du Parc-Royal in the Marais. In the times of the kings of France it was part of the Maison Royale des Tournelles and extended onto what is now Place des Vosges. Large and luxurious, its 2,000 square meters comprised a much larger park, known as Parc Royal. Torn down upon the orders of Catherine de Médicis, street people eventually occupied the area. In time townhouses were built, and the Square bore the name of Léopold Achille, a perfume manufacturer, writer, and member of the city council in the late 1800's and early 1900's.

Although the park is small, it retains the quietness and feeling of that other era. I step inside the Iron Gate and sit on a bench by the grass and dirt path surrounding the square. A long lawn bordered by tall trees, two of which date from the late 1800's and early1900's, is in the center. A play area with a sand box has been added beside the lawn. The square becomes alive with children and their parents or babysitters late in the afternoon. Adults sit on the benches, or the lawn and the children run around. I sit here before the onslaught and it's fun to be able eavesdrop on a French speaking older couple and see a group of twentysomething girls speaking in French and English. I wonder where they live. What sort of lives do they have that they can enjoy such moments, fleeting moments of now that they don't realize will be gone too soon.

I feel displaced and miss my family. What am I doing here?

Then the voice says, "You chose this, you silly woman. Enjoy. Soak in the sun. Walk where you want. There are no clocks. No schedules to keep. You have wanted for years to be here... now. I push myself up and go. I walk the perimeter and find an unexpected, wonderful spot, the 'Jardin de l'Hôtel de Sully.' It turns out to be a shortcut.

Through the busy Rue Saint Antoine to the fancy Place des Vosges. This little hotel was never a hotel but a private residence. As with all residences, gardens or little 'orangeries' (orange gardens) are in the center courtyard hidden from the streets. This piece of paradise has four small square lawns bordered by boxwood hedges. Stone benches dot the paths. I sit with the others who are eating or reading their newspapers. I look up at the sides of this Louis XII mansion and imagine the stories that each window and corridor held through the ages. Perhaps if I were on a tour, the guide would rattle on in a monotone all the pertinent facts and a stream of dates which I would try to comprehend but then would eventually tune out.

The beauty of traveling alone is that I can follow the beat of my own drummer - stop…go…dance.. sit out. As I glance up at the blue sky, red balloons begin to float by. I think of the book <u>The Red Balloon</u> and expect a little boy to appear and chase the balloons. This, however, is part of a spontaneous art installation. They float up everywhere and some get caught in trees or window frames. I marvel at the red against the gray stone of this ancient house.

Then out of the past into the age of consumption, I walk to the Place des Vosges right around the bend. High end store windows of art: bronze rhinoceroses, collages of digital doors, abstract flowers in pale blue and lemon-yellow vases. All – astronomically expensive in euros and over the moon in dollars, but each to one's own taste and pocketbook. I walk on by and continue under the arches of La Place des Vosges. I decide to treat myself not to a rhinoceros but to a lunch. This is Paris after all.

I choose a restaurant and sit at a sidewalk table to watch the Parisians and tourists go by. My soup arrives bubbling with gruyere cheese, accompanied by crusty French bread and glass of red wine. I ordered onion soup not as an American appetizer but for my meal. I hold my glass, lit like rubies in the sunlight, and drain it sip by sip. I decide to splurge on dessert, a tantalizing chocolate mousse and an expresso. I envy my good fortune and health to be here on this perfect day – sun, blue skies, laughter and the chatter of children and adults. Fortified with life and food, I push off to discover more.

Into the nearby Musee Carnavalet, a gem of furniture and artwork, I go to look for 'les toilettes'. Bathrooms are far and few between in Paris and to find ones you don't have to pay for is like finding snow on Miami Beach. In the clean hidden bathrooms, I meet Americans. Birds of a feather who avoid tours and go their own way. They are together in a mini group of two and American Expressing their way through Paris. Coiffured perfectly with blond highlights that only the best salons in New York or Boston can offer, and accessorized with gold jewelry and Hermes scarves, they can turn French heads. We chat. I called it right. One hails from Boston, the other from New York. They are in Paris for a week- free to spend their alimony checks on whatever they wish. High spirited irreverent fiftyish women of entitled means, they invite me to shop with them. I agree but not before we stand in front of the painting of the Latin Quarter in 1958 by Japanese artist Foutija. We become immersed in the streets and clothes of another time and take it as a sign to see if any vintage shops exist in the Marais.

Out of my league in terms of spending capacity, I nonetheless hop aboard the shopping excursion. By now my feet are sore and my legs ache. I did not taxi here. I wore sneakers, so American but so necessary.

Do not try to compete with the shoes that French women wear. You're not walking to your corner café in chic boots for an espresso, but for blocks to soak in the sights, smells, and sounds of a city to last you a lifetime or until your next visit. Wear sneakers. Sure, they'll spot you for an American, but you can claim to be Canadian.

Day 3

SEPTEMBER 21

"Your time is limited, so don't waste it living someone else's life.
Don't be trapped by dogma – which is living with the results of
other people's thinking. Don't let the noise of other's opinions
drown out your own inner voice. And most important, have the
courage to follow your heart and intuition. They somehow already
know what you truly want to become. Everything else is secondary."

STEVE JOBS

I decide to turn the other way this morning – to the Allee Verte toward the Rue Richard Lenoir. Walking down toward the Bastille I see women with market baskets – rather like our small suitcases on wheels but these are canvas large shopping bags on collapsible wheels. All are on a mission to buy the best produce, fish, and meat for their families or just for themselves. I see a curly haired boy with his grand-mere. He is dressed in an orange sweatshirt with a 'loup' or wolf in the front and in one hand he holds a green plastic dinosaur and with the other, his grandmother's hand. I think of my grandson and his small hand in mine – such a moment to remember – the moments that are most important. I never had a grandmother, so I enjoy making memories with him. I think, 'Will he remember me when he is old? And will I see him grow into a man with children of his own? I want to take him to Paris. He loves everything

French from the Eiffel Tower to French bread to Nutella to Monet. His enthusiasm extends to everything life offers.

Where the end of the street meets the circle around the Bastille, the market spreads out. Display upon display form a rectangular covered by a canopy of trees and bordered by tall stone apartment buildings with skinny iron balconies and lace paneled window frames. Heavenly to walk in the sun and stop at each food artistically displayed as only the French can do. Vegetables at one merchant – fruit at another – all lined up in rows or little towers.

.

"Un sac, Madame," a merchant says as he hands me a paper bag. Each vegetable goes in a different sack which he weighs on a digital scale and then writes the price on a piece of brown paper.

"Je commence avec les tomates." I say as I put two fat ripe red tomatoes in one bag and then move on to the little boxes of mushrooms.

"Tous les types de champignons," he says and then begins to explain in what region each type of mushroom is found. And the taste "doux, sale, piquant" sweet, salty, spicy – all of this fascinates me because of the nuances of the expressions and knowledge one can pick up in day-to-day dialogue that you can have with a produce man or woman. I feel like Anthony Bourdain. No conversation exists at Stop and Shop or Big Y when I pick up a saran wrapped bunch of bananas or a plastic covered box of mushrooms.

I don't even like tomatoes or mushrooms, but maybe in Paris they will taste different. I'll be a rebel and put them in an omelet or salad. I feel adventurous when I travel with no one telling me what to get or what to like or dislike. I can do whatever I want. I do not have to put anyone else's opinions into the equation. Just mine, and now in this moment they are the only ones that count. Iced glassy eyed fish and shellfish catch my Interest.

"Madame, you can tell by the eyes of the fish if they are fresh and healthy."

I go, eye to eye, with the rows of fish sorted by type from small to large. I decide on a fat pink and white flounder.

"Parfait madame, Vous avez choisi un beau poisson'

So, he wraps the handsome fish in wax paper and places it in a plastic bag and twills in round and then knots the plastic cord..." Et voilà un limon pour vous'. He hands me a large lemon.

« Cuisinez avec beaucoup de beurre et limon. »

He sounds like Julia with the butter. So, I'll cook it like her, the more butter the better.

Tall and robust, he turns to greet three regulars. They smile at him – one of the middle aged-women points to octopuses with perfect tentacles and fat pinkish bodies. I see no eyes, but I'm not bending down to check. They – the women not the octopuses - know what they are doing.

I dare to ask, "How does one cook 'Une poulpe?'"

"Delicatement," delicately he says.

The women laugh too loudly. The man hands the woman her octopus and turns to me. He intricately explains how to boil the water etc. etc. I feel almost obliged to buy une poulpe but non. This I certainly do not like - Paris or not. Its disgusting mushy mass will not cross my lips.

What entices me are the croissants at the next stand – a young Jeanne Moreau wraps up the one I select, and the plump trio like the 'Dames de Belleville', edge next to me. I ask the merchant if she sells coffee. She shakes her head no with the typical pout, but I continue and ask if anyone sells coffee in the market. "J' sais pas" and a shake of the head conveys 'I don't know'.

I explain that in our farmers' markets coffee, hot chocolate, and lemonade are sold. The mean girls laugh like it is such a ridiculous concept, and one chooses to put in her two cents 'seulement interieur d'un café,' only inside a café.

The fish man has been eavesdropping and nods his head to the left and holds up two fingers. I move two booths over and the crepe woman sells me an expresso. I want to turn back and tell the mean girls that they can get cafe at the crepe stand if they wish – but I really have no need to confirm 'I am right'. I can focus on the nice people one meets. Every country has its ungenerous inhabitants.

It makes me think of a story one of my daughters told me about her drive through Alabama on a hot humid day. She pulled her Connecticut plated Volvo and her dog over to a country store and bought a bottle of water then pointed to the lake across the way – "Can I swim there?" The woman started to say yes, and Rebecca began to unleash her dog. Then the woman became more obliging. She added in a southern drawl – "You could, but I wouldn't. There's alligators in them there waters."

I feel the French woman could have added a comment to make her answer more palatable– "we usually don't , but maybe further down there's 'un fou'/ a crazy French person that sells coffee outside", 'a l'exterieur.'

Under the white tents, the smells of saucissons, Chinese vegetables, and couscous entice me. I gather more provisions for the next few days. The markets have become my regular shopping places. Every Tuesday and Sunday I buy what I need for the next few days. Like the French, I begin to establish a rapport with the sellers.

Day 4

SEPTEMBER 22

"The first condition of understanding a foreign country is to smell it."

RUDYARD KIPLING

Each morning I put my bed away. I fold up the couch, make a pot of strong coffee and open the doors to my secret garden – rather like Miss Havisham's in Great Expectations – all crazy with weeds and dead flowers. A bit of greenery is here and there, and one rose is just starting to bloom in the warm September sun. The smell of Paris hits me every morning – inexplicable but wonderful - it smells of home, a home I never had. I was a beach girl. The smell of the ocean has such an allure for me. Paris is different but equally memorable to my soul.

I spend another morning sitting at my table with a fresh 'cousson aux pommes' that tastes a bit like my mother's apple pie. The sun sweetens the overcast Parisian sky. My mother would have liked it here. I look up at the window; it's not open today, and the sounds of Sinatra do not float in the air.

This flat lies in the 11th a few blocks over from the 3rd, 4,th and 12th. I can walk into any one of those arrondissements within 10 minutes. I try to have each day blossom anew, but I do plan a destination – something, some place I want to see since I have to take a few metro stops to get to wherever it is I desire. Over my coffee and pastry, I pursue the maze of the metro map and check out the beginning and end destination of the numbered lines I have to take. I don't want to be one of those tourists that whip out the map in the middle of the path of people rushing to the turnstiles of the metro. I want to just glance at the signs posted in the underground and follow them. The trick is to always look assured and move forward with purpose. One can always turn around.

By 11:30 the sky is blue and the sun spreads over the garden. Today will be a walk day. The Ile Saint Louis in the 4th is my destination. I'll walk over Avenue Beaumarchais into the Marais and pass my special park square Leopold Achille and further on to the Hotel de Ville which is the town hall not a hotel. Notre Dame is nearby on the Ile de la Cite, and I hear her bells that have been ringing for eight hundred years. In the past I had bought a cross embedded with her birthstone for my college roommate. I have no one who would appreciate such a cross now, so I travel over the Pont d'Arcole, the bridge Arcole, onto this little island which was the beginning of Paris more than 2,000 years ago.

The banks of the waters that surround the island provided a natural defense from the warring Celtic Tribes. From one tribe, the Parisii, the city eventually got its name. Ile de la Cite is shaped like a boat and is crossed by a few bridges. It's the home of Notre Dame, Palais de Justice, Saint Chappelle known for its magical stained glass and perfect Gothic architecture, and La Concergerie, a prison which held the likes of Marie Antoinette and others waiting to be hauled off to the Guillotine during the French Revolution. I do not wish to stand in the long lines today. I can come back. I have the luxury of time.

I skirt past Notre Dame and follow the music and a stray dog over the Pont Saint Louis to wander this tinier quieter island known as Ile des Vaches, the island of cows. This swampy land served as pastureland for cows. Over the centuries it was covered over and replaced by elegant hotels, private residences for the wealthy 17th century notables. Then the revolution decapitated them. Today, the rich still live here.

Two quays, sea wall embankments, go around the island and one main street cuts through the middle to keep the essence of a village. I walk down the main street of Ile Saint Louis and check out the little tourist shops that catch my eye. I enter one that has expensive accessories and clothes on the ground floor, art on the second and a café on the third. With no intention of buying these expensive pieces I pick up a pair of jeweled very Yoko Onoish sunglasses, decorated with pink bling around the lenses and stem. I try on dark lenses with black frames and a tortoise shelled one with lighter lenses. I ask the salesgirl which one she prefers. We both decide on the tortoise ones, and I entertain the idea how fabulous these would look at the Cannes Film Festival with a leopard draped cowl neck gown with a deep bare back. Then reality sets in. I can't wear these to my suburban supermarket. I'd break them in my purse or leave them on a shelf. Besides, the 250 Euro price tag is way too steep.

"I'll think about it. It's a hard decision; they are both so beautiful." I say as I take my lovely time and wander in and out of these enchanting boutiques that one would need a fat wallet and an empty suitcase to take all the purchases home.

Around the corner I walk onto Quai de Bourbon. The Seine rushes by and few people are on the sidewalk. I pass by little gates and doors that mark the private courtyards from 17th Century homes – rented now and owned by the rich. There is an aura of exclusivity here. Slowly, I soak in the feeling of times gone by. One can almost hear the hooves of horses and the rumblings of carriages across these cobble stone streets. I cross to the other side near the tall stone buildings that line the street, a plaque on one stands out — *in the memory of Camille Claudel 1864-1943.* Camille Claudel, lover and apprentice of the great August Rodin, never got credit during her lifetime for her work. The sculptures, the Thinker and the Kiss, are said to be hers.

She lived and worked here on the first floor. She pulled clay out of the underground caverns of the Seine and sculptured it into art. Many of his works were attributed to her, but not before she went mad. Distraught with his treatment of her and society's condemnation, she became ill. Her family institutionalized her. She died in madness.

I think about the ordeals she must have faced by choosing the life of an artist rather than the conventions of the women of those times. Her death came 1943, one of the coldest winters in Paris when little food or fuel existed during the German occupation.

World War ll has been over for more than sixty-five years. I am lucky to be here now. It's warm, and I have clarity of mind. Famished, I enter a tea salon. And spot the epitome of "See that girl with the red dress on…" However, she is not dancing and she's not a girl. In her late fifties — or early 60's; she is dressed in a red tight-fitting sheath with a deep V in the back. A silver zipper traverses her well-shaped back all the way to mid-calf She moves with grace and focus over her group of tourists and regulars.

"Bienvenue," she welcomes me and gestures to a table near the window. She must be the owner of this tea Salon on Ile Saint Louis. I join the islands of tables inhabited by singles, couples, and families. With agility she moves among their tables. It's getting hot. She runs her fingers through her white spiky short hair as she keeps an eye on the door.

She stops taking an order and walks to the lattice metal door to open it for a young boy and his 'aged' grand-mere. "Tu veux t'asseoir mon petit?'

«Oui, » he says that he wishes to sit down.

"Voila Madame" she indicates the larger table between the door and the window.

The elderly woman nods yes, and the 'owner' helps her to the chair and bends down to tie her black shoelaces. With loving care, she secures a double knot and caresses the woman's gnarled hand. The gesture speaks to the old women we will all be one day.

Taking their order first, she brings the boy a carafe of water and two glasses then returns with a cup of hot tea for his grand-mere/ grandmother.

This scene goes unnoticed by the table of Americans next to me. The teenage daughter is engrossed with texting and is oblivious to the sights, smells, and people of Pairs. The husband and wife are having a dispute concerning directions and where to go next.

I sit alone with my glass of red house wine and a gruyere cheese filled galette folded meticulously with a fried egg on top and smile to myself. "I'm glad I'm free to wander and get lost without anyone berating me for it."

Day 5

SEPTEMBER 23

A woman past forty should make up her mind to be young not her face.

Today I exit without my strong coffee. I'm going to see if I can get an expresso and croissant. The walk is long and quiet except for delivery trucks and vendors going in and out of shops. I say 'bonjour' to the occasional sidewalk sweeper. I pass through part of the Marais, cross in front of the Hotel de Ville, Notre Dame and then over a bridge to Saint Louis. I walk down the main street of Ile Saint Louis and down to yesterday's café, the Cafe Meditarranee to see 'that girl with the red dress on'. I see the ferme/closed sign - no breakfast crowd, she serves lunch and afternoon tea for the tourists and neighborhood customers. However, the door is open, and I see the waitress/owner and today's dress du jour. It is pink lace – tight with a V in the back and a silver zipper traversing her back and derriere. This must be her signature look. I love it -sexy, forceful and with a definite presence. Her face with a slash of red on her lips has strength and beauty. Her white spikey hair makes me think she might be in her sixties. What I know is that she does not spend her time making up her face but rather her mind and attitude.

I walk back to the Seine and sit for an expresso and a croissant at a café with a river view and a price tag to match. I plan my route to

Montmartre and my buying agenda. After seeing her red dress yesterday and her pink lace today I want to buy some fabric or "tissu' as the French say. I enjoy sewing and getting unique fabric to match up with the garment I want to make. I'm not a seamstress but simple patterns I can manage from my days in junior high school when they called it home economics. Why that name is beyond me? I never learned about finances just the money involved in planning a menu and buying the ingredients. Even in the 60's it was referred to as 'housewife' chores. Forget about the stock market or setting up your financial future instead we were taught how to sew as though we were frontier women of another era. I performed abysmally. We had to follow directions to the letter of the law since the chunky shirtwaist dressed Mrs. Marmaline would swoop in with her scissors and 'stitch puller outer gadget' and wreak havoc on my work. She made me pin the darts and seams and then base stitch them before I could sew them for real. She would pull out all the stitches as she mumbled under her breath, "I can't believe this. A chicken could peck her way over darts and seams better than this girl." When she handed back my garment, it was dotted with pin holes and pulled threads. I hated that class, and my grade reflected it.

You may ask, "How can she sew and why does she even want to?" My mother was the reason for my minimal success. She had read about classes that simplified the technique of sewing clothes. She signed me up. Eight lessons which would ensure the creation of making a dress, a suit, and a pair of pants. I was in my glory with minimal pinning, no basting, and no use of chalk and a marking wheel. I like to improvise and estimate things (probably why geometry was not a favorite either), so at the end of eight weeks I had my garments – a green tweed suit with a gold silky lining, a cranberry corduroy A line dress, and black wool lined trousers. My mother said I was the cat's meow, an expression I had never heard before, but it made me feel good. As the years passed, my mother's investment paid off.

I made curtains, slipcovers, work outfits, maternity clothes, baby clothes, and even adjusted my mother's clothes when she became old.

Fast forward decades and I am now obsessed with Project Runway. On a trip to New York City, I even went to Mood. Compared to the T.V. show, the store seemed small and disorganized; I did not even see Swatch, the Boston Terrier, but the aura permeated the shop.

Of course, I am going to check out Paris' fabric stores. Paris, the fashion capital of the world, is the perfect place for fabric as well as fashion. I want to see what the French fabric stores have. My creations will remind me of my journey here. My trusty metro map indicates the stop at Anvers right off Rue de Dunkerque or Abesses at the base of Sacre Coeur. I choose Abesses.

As I ascend the steep winding stairs leading up and out of Abesses, I am enclosed by circular murals on the walls. Artists from Montmartre have made murals which depict times from the past and the present. You need a strong heart and legs. No high heels since the steps are steep and the cobble stones of Montmartre are a test in themselves! Ladies if you need a knee or hip replacement, have it done a year before your trip or get an Uber or taxi to take you to Montmartre. It's not called 'Mont' (the hill) of the martyr for nothing. It's not for sissies.

I follow the base of the sidewalks beneath Sacre Coeur and come to Place Pierre and its side streets which are lined with fabric shops: La Reine, Frou-Frou Marche Saint Pierre, Jansens & Jansens. The inside is packed with bolts and bolts of unique fabrics which flow outside onto the sidewalks. The window displays are extraordinary. Fabric, mannequins, piles of accessories and at this time of year Halloween creations. It's September and Halloween is around the corner.

Before I enter, the tables outside entice. The bolts are priced and stacked in categories with handwritten signs indicating the price per meter not yard. Perfectly sized silk and polyester remnants for a foulard (scarf) which the French seem to wear as a mandatory accessory are stacked on a little square table by the door. I select a few in black, white, navy, and white. With a foulard draped around my neck, I can blend in like Vinnie in <u>My Cousin Vinnie</u>. In the film Joe Pesci tries a similar tactic with a leather jacket. I, however, am more successful until the French glance at my shoes which do not blend in, but I do not care. I cross the threshold with my big American sneakered feet.

I enter each store with its rooms of bolts and bolts of fabric lined up on tables according to colors. I feel like the Project Runway contestants, but I do not have any idea of what to buy. I have no design sketch from which to select the perfect fabric, and all the variety distracts me. In the corners of the rooms are mannequins or rather bizarre large dolls in outrageous outfits. They resemble the Joker or at best the carney dolls of Coney Island. Clowns with large red mouths and ruffled collars in red, white, and black checks with bodies draped in shiny red or white puffy shirts and harem pants are hooked to the walls. Then there are the witches in beaded black or shimmering gray swathed in lace. They remind me of Charles Dickens' reclusive character Miss Havisham in Great Expectations who dwells in her lace wedding dress amidst rooms crowded with cobwebs and a decaying wedding cake.

Yes, rather like a fun house, but it's cool. I wander from table to table touching the fabrics and looking at all the varieties of colors and patterns. So unusual – including the labels of origin– Tunisia, Spain, France, Morocco, India. I decide on a harvest gold fabric with a green swirl. It is heavy broadcloth cotton.

"Madame, that's perfect for pillows and upholstering."

"Yes, you must have read my mind. My daughter-in-law is from Spain, and she loves these colors."

"Mais oui", this fabric is from Spain. How many pillows and what size?"

"Two. About this size" I hold up my hands to indicate the approximate size.

"OK. I cut for you." She lifts the bolt up and takes it over to a cutting table. Expertly she glides the scissors across the fabric. Two perfect squares are then folded up and pinned with a slip of paper with the price of 6.8 euros.

She takes the remnants from my hands and folds those up and attaches another price slip of 5 euros. "Anything else Madame?"

"Yes, linen for a dress." While looking around, I get a Tim Gunn 'Make it work' moment. I ask the saleswoman for some paper and a pencil.

I sketch a dress – a simple square neckline, sleeveless and straight-below the knee but not mid-calf and of course the back is a V. I would place the zipper on the side not down the back – too tough to zip up.

It reminds me of a Vogue pattern I have in my sewing box from the 1970's and of course the marvelous owner of the Café Med. I want nothing clingy but something in an edgier abstract or geometric design in black and white that skims my hips.

Day 6

SEPTEMBER 24

"Two roads diverged in a wood, and I – I took the road less traveled by... and that has made all the difference."

ROBERT FROST

The roads you choose mold who and what you will become. I did not take the less traveled path but the conventional one. I have no wild youth nor over the top crazy memories to fuel my old age. Now that I am nearing that age, I regret my too conventional life. If I could have picked and chosen those decisions that would not have killed me or landed me in jail, I would have done so. But my road of responsible hard work is what provided for me and made a difference to my children and my students. I was able to buy food, shelter, and opportunities for my children. Love and fuel for their dreams came with the package. For my students I gave the same love, listened to their aspirations, and tried to show them possibilities. I took my own children and my students to Hartford, New York City, Quebec, Caen, Cannes, Paris... to show them different worlds. Young adults now, I think about their lives and hope I made a difference.

Women especially must be adventurous at any age. Take a journey of the spirit, of the soul. Travel. Make your lunches, bring bottled water, and be prepared. If it sounds like the girl scouts, so be it, but when you are hungry, you'll have the simple food you need. The road of life is hard and people who say life is not fair fail to realize life comes with no guarantees. You make your choices. Maybe you work at it or maybe you do not. At best life is tough; at worst, it is cruel and perhaps tragic. Life deals you a certain hand of cards, and it is how you play them. Therefore, take the cards dealt to you and enjoy. If they are not good, live through it to get to better times. Trust that doors will open, and you will enjoy whatever comes your way. Live worry free; watch for serendipity and expect the best.

Today I am taking a few metro trains to be in the area where Hemingway lived as a young man. He used to walk through the Luxembourg Gardens in the 7th arrondissement. I will follow in his footsteps. He was a man who had a wife who supported him emotionally and financially. He was able to rent a separate room in which to write and when he wanted a change of pace, he wrote and drank in cafes and bars. His opportunities and acceptance were greater than any woman's would have been. Writing was a job that he took seriously. His goal was to be a writer of merit, and he had a woman to support him and even edit his work.

As I meander through the Luxembourg Gardens past the fountains and up the pathway bordered by statues, I smell the still warm air of September as the leaves begin to turn. Soon they will be crunching under other travelers' feet as they did for Hemingway in the 1920's.

The cemetery I want to visit is on the other side of this garden. I let myself wander down the paths to the Cimitiere de Montparnasse. Perhaps the dead can teach me something about the living. Each day is an opportunity to learn about ourselves and others. We women no matter what our age must set goals and make our own opportunities – fearless and independent mindsets are necessary.

When I walk up to the sidewalk on the other side, I become uncertain. An older George Clooney in a grey suit, black shoes and very 1940's hat says, "Madame je peux vous aider?"

"Oui, s'il vous plait, I can use some help." He walks me to the cemetery. And says "Bonne Journee, Madame."

I walk around an iron fence to a gate which leads to mini roads, bordered by dirt lined paths leading to the headstones of the famous and not so famous. Trees hang overhead and shelter the likes of playwright Eugene Ionesco, poet Charles Baudelaire, philosophers Simone de Beauvoir and Jean-Paul Sartre. At the end of one path is a small statue of Liberty marking the way to Frederic August Bartholdi, the man who sculptured our Statue of Liberty and put his mother's face as the face of freedom and justice for the oppressed. All the monuments are huddled together. Do they listen to us talk? Do they ask why we are spending time with the dead when there is so much living to do?

The warm sunlight splatters the paths leading to clusters of tombstones, mini cities within a city. Some are commemorated with pots of geraniums, impatiens, ferns and even planted roses and lilies. A sad stone woman with hands folded under her chin and crossed legs rests on one flat stone and a flying angel rests on a tomb of a standing stone. Crosses and Jewish stars grow between the stones. I am not alone. I look up. A dignified man with salt and pepper hair, jogs among the dead in a black tracksuit. An odd place to jog I think, but perhaps he thinks I'm odd to eat lunch in a cemetery. I sit on a bench next to Baudelaire, the poet, and take out my camembert, tomato and basil sandwich on a baguette and sip water from my REI bottle. You know that question they ask celebrities – "Who would you invite to your dinner party?" Is the answer Beyoncé, Alex Rodrigues, Adam Levine etc.? My initial question would be different. Who would you share lunch with on a city bench? I'd leave out the cemetery part.

In front of his tomb are two artificial flowerpots and one live green stalked plant. Recent admirers left them since he's been dead for almost two hundred years. Through all those years, lovers of his poetry lived by his words. His poem, 'Enivrez-vous' spoke to me when I was young.

"Enivrez-vous...Be drunk **Be drunk with the joy of life and living...**"

From the time I read those lines many years have passed. Where did they go? What I know is that I am not the same person now as I was then. A black crow flies and sits on a statue in front of me. I take it as a sign to move on to adventures that lie ahead. With a last swig of water, I bid adieu to Baudelaire. I know the paths to lead me out onto the streets of beeping horns, people talking, and children riding tricycles. The sun beats down and warms me. I will wander wherever my legs carry me.

Tomorrow is my birthday.

I pass by a market where bunches of sunflowers cascade from vases. I select a fresh lovely bouquet.

"Les tournesols s'il vous plait," I say. I love that word 'tourne' for turn and 'sol' for 'soleil'. It means they turn toward the sun, and that's exactly what sunflowers do in the fields. They turn their heads up to the sun.

The man at the market answers. "Oui mademoiselle, les fleurs de Van Gogh."

That makes me feels young – a mademoiselle and not Madame. I shall be like the sunflower and turn by face toward the sunlight and live in the glow of the present.

What also amazes me is that this produce man knows his French culture. Do you think the guy in Stop and Shop would know who Van Gogh was or even his own American painter, Andrew Wyeth?

$\mathcal{D}ay$ 7

SEPTEMBER 25 – MY BIRTHDAY

You don't choose the day you enter the world, and you don't choose the day you leave. It's what you do in between that makes all the difference."

– ANITA SEPTIMUS

"You make me feel so young..."

I woke up the earliest this day maybe because I was waiting for a different feeling. I stretch on my sofa bed and look toward the sliding doors that are draped with two sheer lace panels of flowers and butterflies. It's light outside. I know it's morning even though the outside garden walls are so high that they cut out the sky.

I am different. For the first time in my life, I am alone – no longer surrounded by family, roommates, friends, and children. One goes from a protected childhood to protecting one's own children. I think of my mother who would always promise Indian summer days for my birthday – warm and sunny September 25th days. I push myself up from the sofa bed, open the doors and look up at the sky between and over the stone apartment buildings. The sky is blue and the air warm. It will be a day like our mothers tell us about and that we really do not remember until we are mothers ourselves or until we reach the age to wonder who our mothers really were, and what they actually thought.

48

During my junior high and high school years my mother lived alone and so it continued long after I was on my own. She was alone most of her life. I know there is a difference between being alone and being lonely. I wonder now if at times she was overcome by loneliness. I suspect the answer is yes. I do know that she was up for adventure, and if she had the money, she would have traveled around the world. After she retired, she traveled with her best friend and took courses at universities. She approved of my work ethic and the trips I took with my students. She would have loved to be here in Paris on my birthday – perhaps telling me things about her youth and secrets of her past which I never knew.

If lilacs were in season, I would have bought them – those were her favorites and mine next to sunflowers. I put a square glass vase of 'tournesols' on my bistro table with my coffee and croissant. I wait to hear Sinatra again from the window across the way, but it is shut. I would be ecstatic if old blue eyes crooned 'You make me feel so young... Perhaps that would have happened for real if I had lived in the 1940's, but today I'll have to settle for being young at heart and try to be somewhat fearless like youth.

The other day I found a 'centime' on the sidewalk – A 'centime' is worth less than a penny and they don't make or even use them anymore. No French franc denominations exist. The universal euro has replaced all, but I slid it into my jean pocket. Ever since my mother died, I believe she leaves me pennies. She told me once that her mother used to put pennies in a drawer for her to spend when she was little. When she was old, she would stoop to pick up pennies It's a habit I now do because I believe it's a sign that she's watching over me. There could be nothing on the table in my house or in my locker at the gym and then when I return a penny is there. So today she left me a French penny for my birthday.

With such serendipity, I am off to another part of Montmartre. Full of spirit and determination, I shall be like 'Amelie' in the movie of the same name. I promised myself a birthday lunch at Le Café des Deux Moulins where the movie was filmed. Montmartre is high above central Paris, in the area that used to be farmland and vineyards. The hill or 'le mont' of Montmartre was dotted with 'moulins' or windmills when the likes of such artists as Toulouse Lautrec, Renoir, Degas, Utrillo and Picasso lived there in the 19th – century. It is far away from my studio apartment on the right bank of the Seine.

Too far to walk, I'll save my steps for all the hilly streets of Montmartre. Three metro lines later I enter La Rue le Pic where the café Les Deux Moulins is located.

Up the hill and on a corner, the restaurant sits quietly on its haunches. It emits no crazy busy windmill vibes. However, once inside it's a jolt into the past with its shabby décor of a provincial grandmother's kitchen with old lace curtains and overstuffed chairs, yet mixed in is a 1950 zinc bar counter, Belle Époque gold speckled mirrors, 1930's art deco airplane propeller fans creating a 1940's/50's Edward Hopper vibe. I sit to the left at a table near the window but with a view of the bar's gold faucets and zinc countertop.

A photo of Amelie is on the wall, and I have the waiter take a photo of me with her. If she were real, she would be too timid in person to pose with me. The café seems empty without her presence. I order a tray of various cheeses and red wine. Bread arrives of course, and I toast my glass of red wine to Amelie's photo and to her inquisitive nature. She grabbed hold of a slice of serendipity which led to a boyfriend and down the streets of Montmartre on his motorcycle. A boyfriend would be interesting - a bit of romance – but the motorcycle - non. That much adventure I am not up for.

After lunch I want a nap, but instead I leave and climb further up the hill. I find a park where a shirtless man in shorts is sunning himself on the grass on this cream puff blue sky day. Could be a chance meeting if I fell over him or stepped on him, but he's far from a 'boyfriend type and far too young. Instead, I approach a grey cat lying by a lamp post. He occasionally rolls in the dirt – the cat not the man- as a flock of pigeons two feet away peck at crumbs.

An older couple sit on a bench and share lunch. A grandmother plays with her grandbaby and keeps up a stream of dialogue for him. I miss those intimate moments of life. Workers sweep with their brooms and empty the trash baskets on posts a few feet off the ground. Typical things done every day around the world, but today I watch more closely since it's my birthday, and it is Paris after all.

"I love it here. I want to stay forever...I will write here. I will live and write alone. And each day I will see a little more of Paris, study it, learn it as I would a book. The streets sing, the stores talk, the houses drip history, glory, romance."

These are not my words, but they could be. No, Henry Miller wrote them in the 1920's.

I've always wished for a time machine to take me to those places and times that touch my heart. Before Henry Miller's era I would have liked to know the times of the Belle Époque – the last part of the 19th century when Renoir walked up from the park where I now sit, crossed the Place Du Tertre and down the side streets to his house on Rue Corot. The Musee de Montmartre now houses his gardens. I pass the building and wonder where his room was, where he painted and which artists would come to visit. Maybe Pissarro or Modigliani would walk with him on the promise of a glass of wine and a convivial chat in the garden by the house. Since Pierre Auguste is not home today, I go inside the Musee de Montmartre to learn about the rough and realistic times of Montmartre. The liberal community of artists who exchanged ideas and political viewpoints lived here in poverty and dirt. It was not 'la vie en rose' - not a romantic period. In truth, it was a terrible time - a time before vaccines, penicillin, and sanitation.

The vineyard garden holds the last blooms of summer. I sit on the swing and ask a young woman to take my picture. No selfies for me as I stand up on the swing and hold its ropes in each hand like Renoir's portrait of the girl in blue who stood up on the swing with the path behind and her blue dress dabbled in sunlight. People work and September is not the high tourist season. My only company is a silky black cat sitting next to me on the bench. Plump and satisfied, he takes advantage of the sunlight as I do before the winds of fall and the snow of winter descend.

To be separated from the ones I love makes me sad, and at times the price is too high, but the present is all I have. I need to write, walk, and breathe in these hills of Paris. For all we ever have at any age is the moment.

To travel alone is to be free of constraints – sure no one encourages you, but no one constrains you. I know I will be too old one day to climb the flight of steps from the Rue Foyatier to the upper part of Montmartre. I'll be taking the funicular which runs alongside. For now, it's my test for my legs and spirit. It makes me feel young although I can no longer bound up two at a time, but the view from the top is spectacular. My heart and

legs hold out as I come to this spot where I can see over the rooftops and down to side cafes. I gaze out over all of Paris. I just stand, look and remember to breathe.

The trek down is almost as difficult - from la Rue du Cardinal-Dubois and down the steep downhill steps to the school Henri IV at the base. I hear music and spot an accordionist in front of the school. The melody of La vie en Rose filters up as students bound down the steps behind me singing that song of Edith Piaf's. I hum as they pass me by. The teenagers reach the bottom before me and dance and sing in front of the accordionist. They leave a few euros in his hat.

I hope they find and live 'la vie en Rose". I am happy that song still resonates with the young. I put money in his hat for the wonderful birthday serenade. I smile as I think of a life with rose colored glasses. Before hopping onto the metro, I see a young woman selling hats from a cart at the bottom. I join the small crowd around her and select a few hats to try on.

"You must buy that one." A dark- haired woman tells me.

"Oui, parfait", her daughter echoes. She is wearing the same hat in navy. Mine is caramel brown. It is a cloche with a brim decorated with felt flowers and a half veil mysteriously shading the eyes. I feel like Ingrid Berman from Casablanca – or an Agatha Christie detective collaborating with Inspector Poirot in the 1920's or 30's.

I adore hats and have too many. Some women obsess about shoes – for me it's hats. Where will I wear it? Such is my mantra because how many things do I need. I tell them it's my birthday, and in unison they all say, "buy it". It's made for you."

So of course, I do, and whenever I wear it, I will think of that special day in Paris – a day with Amelie, Jean Paul, and Ingrid. No tour could have brought me these experiences only the adventuring and wandering by oneself. "You'll always have Paris."

"Yes, I will.

$\mathcal{D}ay\,8$

SEPTEMBER 26

"If you are lucky enough to have lived in Paris as a young man, then wherever you go for the rest of your life it stays with you. For Paris is a moveable feast"

ERNEST HEMINGWAY

I think of these words often; not because I'm a Hemingway want-to-be, but I am envious that he was here during that glorious time between the two world wars. His macho style never appealed to me, or his simple - Spartan use of words. I know they resounded at the time – his writing style was new and fresh. I do admire that he worked at it. I do not admire how he let his family and friends fall by the wayside so he could pursue what he wanted.

Men were/are accorded that road, women not so much. What I envy about Hemingway was his luck to be in the right place... at the right time. Imagine the freedom of the 1920's in Paris. The war to end all wars had ended. Prohibition did not exist. Living in Paris was cheap. Hemingway tells us it cost $1,000 a year for lodging, food, wine, expenses, and entertainment. Ideas were expounded and shared. Some of the greatest painters, writers and philosophers lived within blocks or streets of one another.

Today over a one hundred years later, I spread out on my Paris kitchen counter my purchases, my moveable feast, bought from Tuesday, Thursday, and Sunday market areas. I select cheese, fruit, vegetables, and bread to cut up for lunch and snacks. A banana and an apple I place in my satchel munch during my meanderings.

Today I follow the footprints of Ernest not of Hemingway. I want to find the young man, the Ernest of youth who was strong, idealistic, and determined. Reading and rereading his works on Paris, I want to pull back the scrim – that theatrical veil that separates the audience from the actors on stage. Perhaps, if I pull it back, I can step over the apron onto the stage to see the Paris of 1923 when Ernest was but a quarter of a century old,

I expect to see them when I step off the metro near Saint Germain des Pres and walk up toward Montparnasse. Those writers and friends of the halcyon days of youth, Hemingway, F. Scott Fitzgerald, Gertrude Stein, James Joyce, the Murphys, and Sylvia Beach from Shakespeare and Company. I look for them in their haunts along Saint Germain des Pres and then down Rue Descartes toward Ernest's apartment at 74 Rue Cardinal Lemoine. I stand in front of the blue door and look at the plaque that marks this residence of the Hemingways. Again, I'm going back in time and wonder which window looked out from his and Hadley's meager kitchen and small cold living room. I know he had a rented room elsewhere to work. In my dream state I hear a woman's voice in English

"Do you want me to take your photo?'

Why didn't she address me in French? After all, I am wearing a scarf!

But I look down at my shoes. Of course, they are not leather, not heels, not chic, but rather my comfortable quick drying REI 'walking for miles shoes' I wear every day.

Her name is Rosa and she's from Australia. Her accent is wonderful. She knows no French nor anything about Hemingway yet was told to see this apartment where he lived in Paris. She's done a world wind tour of

Italy, Spain and now France and will pick up Portugal on the back end. Not really traveling alone, she meets up with friends in various cities. But now she's on her own, and just wants to go back to her hotel, a fairly established one in the area. She's too tired and does not want to go to the cafe around the corner. I would have liked to find out why she travels and have a chat with someone. I can't think of relaxing in a hotel room when there's the entire afternoon and evening to enjoy. All I can think of is this glorious day to walk about Paris – to be a flaneuse. We part. She to rest in her room and I to continue to walk.

Paris has always been a city of 'flaneurs', strollers - not the speed walkers of Central Park in Manhattan. Now I have the time and these warm September days – perfect jewels before the onslaught of winter's snow and interminable gray sky, to be a 'flaneuse'. I remember my Indian summer days of youth. The days just before school opened when we would shop for pencil boxes, Buster Brown shoes, and starched plaid dresses. All these items were necessary for the 'rentrée', the return to school, when a certain smell caressed the air for a soon-to-be new school year and the promises to come.

I have passed several ecoles maternelles, elementary schools, nice stone edifices of learning with playgrounds of swings. They seem like ours but for the plaques affixed on exterior walls – "45 Jewish students were taken by the Nazis on October 9, 1943 and exported to Auschwitz. All forty-five died." The schools differ and the numbers and dates change but the plaques are still stuck on the walls from a time long ago when the unthinkable happened. These inconceivable – but undeniable facts stand witness to what occurred here during the dark years of Paris 1940-44. I read these plaques and cry for those who died then and those who are dying today because history repeats itself. The ugly head of racism and xenophobia rears itself again not just in other parts of the world but in the United States as well.

To clear my head, I decide to walk to Luxembourg Garden again. I head in the direction of La Tour Montparnasse. The tower marks the area of Montparnasse where the writers and artists of Hemingway's day congregated. The hills of Montmartre emptied out as artists and writers migrated to Montparnasse to share ideas and live a simpler life, unhampered by tourists. Hemingway used to pass through Le Jardin du Luxembourg Gardens to get to Montparnasse.

As I walk the pebbled paths through the leafy bough covered way, the flowers are still redolent with summer scents and the grand Bassin, the manmade lake, is surrounded by plant linked terraces and chairs set out for sunbathers and talkers.

I choose to sit on the edge of the Bassin careful not to get splashed by children pushing their sailboats out toward the center where a fountain flushes water into the Bassin. I do what I like to do best – people watch and be silent to listen to the laughter and conversations that abound. "I think of those children 70 years ago during the Dark Years. How much laughter existed– then?

I am getting tired of baguettes and to tell the truth - croissants – hard to believe but true. As I walk towards the Tower in the distance and under massive trees, I see one that has turned reddish orange and I wonder how it would feel to shuffle my feet through the fallen leaves of late October. Next time I need to include that... so cheese sandwiches and fewer restaurant lunches and dinners stateside would ensure the opportunity to return.

All the thoughts about World War II make me want to see the Jean Moulin Museum. I believe the people who lived during the years of War live their lives in the present. The daily acts of life were intensified – to cook, to eat, and to hold one's loved ones were not a given. The next day could tear it all away. To dream of the future probably gave them hope to continue on with the excruciating hardships of constant hunger, cold, and fear. Choices were made to turn and run or to stay and fight. Jean Moulin was a public official, an artist, and a resistance fighter. He was one who turned to fight and paid the ultimate price. The museum is dedicated to him and framed by stories of General Leclerc, Charles de Gaulle, the allies, and many other men and women who decided to act and take back their freedom. They put their lives in peril every day in order to break the iron grip of Nazi tyranny.

I walk toward the signs for Montparnasse and ask people on the street where is the museum? No one knows about it. Three hours of getting lost leads me to a clothing store – rather like an H&M. I have a brief conversation with a young man who learned his English from a year in Toronto. He said, "You Americans are interested in history." He was rather ashamed that he never went to learn about Jean Moulin who eventually was captured and tortured by the notorious Klaus Barbie, the Butcher of Lyon. Jean Moulin escaped only by death in 1943. He did not see the liberation of Paris, a year later in August of 1944. This young salesman I'm speaking with was born probably 45 years later.

"Í go to see it after work one day," he says. I sense that he means it. He pours over my map to no avail and then checks out the store's iPad – helping customers in between his searches. He discovers it is less than a block away, but it involves some curves and crossovers. He leads me out onto the sidewalk and walks me across the square and then indicates how far to go and the turns to arrive at the entrance of Le musee de Jean Moulin. I thank him, and he says "no, thank you for liberating my city and my France." It feels nice to take credit for being an American in these political times set in another millennium, so far removed from those times.

Jean Moulin was just a man whose normal upbringing and nature did not indicate what his life would hold. His museum transports one back to a time when people had to sacrifice and work together to survive. Today we need more human contact and conversation to allow the fissures of our eggshell existence to crack open the heart.

Day 9

SEPTEMBER 27

"The traveler was active; he went strenuously in search of people, of adventure, of experience. The tourist is passive; he expects interesting things to happen to him; he goes sight-seeing."

DANIEL BOORSTEIN

I pass in a parallel reality among those who have a purpose: those who work, shop, go to school or vacation from another place closer than the U.S. They have a life here or elsewhere with parents, young children, husbands, wives etc. I have lived that. It is not good to feel sorry for myself. Sheer stupidity - We can never have all things, all people, and all places at the same time. Judy Collins' song 'Turn, turn, turn..." plays in my head. Time is a continuum like an airport walkway on which you get on and off.

I recognize this in me. I need to be that traveler who dives into new experiences not the tourist who just views things from the outside. I need some activities that interest me where I can meet people since I am alone, and frankly, why am I second guessing myself? A woman alone does not go into bars and chat up those hanging around. At least I don't. I do have the confidence and a feeling of security to go to coffee counters with barstools or cafes or stand next to someone to observe a painting at a museum or grab a jar of jam at Monoprix, a very refined Walmart, and perhaps comment or say hello, but I'm not an extrovert. And in reality, the French don't chit chat. They don't start conversations with random strangers.

One of my daughters signed me up for two mini courses. She knows me. She booked me into making bread and eating chocolate. This is now on my agenda. I can mingle with other travelers and these adventures have an end result – yummy baguettes and croissants to eat. I journeyed to the 12th to a little bakery – a boulangerie. Again, I feel like Julia Childs not because of my ability but because like her – I like to eat and possibly because I am taller than everyone else in the class including the baker, Didier, but not the guide, Roberto, a distinguished tall thin gentleman' d'un certain age' – if that applies to men.

I feel comfortable listening to his English and French. He had been a lawyer but decided to become a tour guide because he likes meeting people. That too is why I am here. He was from Haiti but has a Swiss Italian background. Well educated – I find it funny how people tell you things in these one-time only encounters they would never tell you at a casual party. His sister has serious health and financial difficulties, but she has been lucky enough to have a friend helping her. As a gift of appreciation, he wants to take the friend to Switzerland where he and his sister grew up. His sister has had a tragic life and he wants to show his appreciation for the love and care the friend has given her. I listen to his honest story. I like that he told me. The others in the class have not arrived so we have time.

The baker, Didier, speaks no English and seems more like a soccer player – strong arms and legs, solid chest, and a frank demeanor. Although he has always been a baker, he is unable to eat what he makes now. He's become allergic to flour and milk products – so gluten free and lactose free he must be.

All the students have arrived. Three Americans from California traveling together, a pair of Japanese women, and the other three single ones: one from Canada, one from the Philippines, named Elizabeth, who says her mother-in-law who is 97 is finally accepting her as her son's wife, and me from Connecticut.

We listen in French, English and Japanese as we roll, shape, and make three cuts on the top of the perfect thick cylindrical shape loaves. They need to breathe. Next, we fold the croissants. For two hours we stand around a floured marble top table and do as we are instructed. Roberto translates Didier's French into English, so I get the benefit of hearing it twice. Another translator translates from French into Japanese. Besides taking away a baguette and two croissants I take away a sense of human connection and camaraderie as I breathe in the glorious smell of a French boulangerie.

Sometimes it feels that you connect with people you meet in transit more than with people you have worked with or seen in your town for years. It's that instant connection made while doing something you both appreciate.

I walk toward the metro eating my baguette with no concern for the trail of crumbs I leave for the pigeons of Paris. I have no plans and will get off near the center of Paris. Inside the metro I select my exit spot –Saint Paul. It sounds like a quaint village so Saint Paul it is. Le village of Saint Paul is a beautiful spot lost in time, a Shangri-la within the city of Paris. A labyrinth of cobblestone streets encompasses old shops with antiquated doors and windows. I feel as though I am stepping back into the time when Paris was a medieval village. Located near Hotel de Sens in the 4th arrondissement, le village Saint Paul rests in a secluded walkway off of Rue Saint Paul/Charlemagne behind arched passageways and sits as a parcel of what was.

Now it is converted into shops for artisans. The old stone walls crumble inside the shops. The doors and windows rest ajar because they are too difficult to close. The years have played havoc with hinges and locks. Above the antique, sculpture stores and art shops are little apartments. Many of the stores appear like attics with dusty goods stacked and restacked.

One of the stores on an outside street had a magnificent large watercolor which I liked. The price was reasonable, but I did not want to bother shipping it home. I had no idea where I would hang it in my house. I did not indulge my impulse. In retrospect, I regret not getting it as a memory of a lovely day in St Paul village. It is unfortunate because the store will probably be closed the next time I go. The owner is a British woman who has been in business for thirty years. She said the city of Paris was buying up the area and she would be forced to move to make way for redevelopment.

I continue down the main Rue Saint-Paul and around to the outside to the boisterous Lycee Charlemagne. This smooth honey colored stone building housed the Jesuits centuries ago but in 1804 it was made into a school. Famous graduates include Victor Hugo and Honoré de Balzac, novelists, and Leon Blum and Lionel Jospin, politicians, and Joseph Joffre, Marshal of France. As I pass by these French adolescents talking in groups, shouting across the street, and running into the basketball/soccer court to pick up a ball and play, I wonder which ones will be added to the list of famous graduates. The energy of youth and dreams exclude no nationality.

I stroll by the Hotel de Sens and its beautiful gardens. An old man sits on one bench petting his small scruffy brown dog. Another dog lover, a woman, sits on the opposite side of the garden square with her pug, lying quietly in the sun. She looks at him with adoring eyes before picking up her book to read again. A young couple with their lunch sit squeezed next to one another and share the same soda bottle. They take a bite, murmur, gaze into one another's eyes, and then share the soda as though their lips are touching. Laughter rises from the side of the park by the dirt sidewalk where a group of young men play bocce. They line up empty wine bottles and have contrived a game which is a mélange of American bowling and Italian bocce. Between the throws of the small rubber ball, they take turns having a swig from a half full bottle of red wine. I think of such a game in an American park – but oh no, they would round you up, confiscate all the bottles, and give you a public ordinance mischief fine. For me it is entertainment; no one is pushing me toward yet another museum or another café. When I've had enough, I'll move on. Such is the pleasure of traveling alone.

After my bread making class and listening to human dialogue, I feel as if I have stepped off my island and connected with other travelers in the ocean of life. It is all good. I leave this little park on my own... to journey out once more – this time toward the Seine to enjoy these September skies as perfect jewels before the abrupt assault of winter.

The Seine does not have the salty scent of the sea, the smell of ships and adventure. It is rather dirty, in reality very dirty. I think of the huge catfish that they say lived in these filthy waters. If I fall in, the next stop will be Hotel Dieu, the ancient hospital near Notre Dame. Yes, I'd need God's help to disinfect and shoot me full of antibiotics. Probably some remnant of the plague swirls in those dark tumultuous torrents.

I don't lean over any bridges but follow the avenue sidewalk down toward Pont Neuf, the oldest bridge- not a new bridge- in Paris. It was built in 1607 with no houses lining its edges like the other bridges spanning the Seine in the 1500's. The bouquinnistes (book sellers) are open on these sunny days. Think of an old wooden tool chest the size of a kitchen table which the owners close at night and paddle lock tight until the next morning when it opens like a Fabergé egg – not glittery but marvelously filled with old books.

I'd like to buy a book from one of these book sellers. On my first trip to Paris as a teenager I bought a yellow paperback book of poetry by Baudelaire – not that I could really read it, but 5 francs bought me a piece of Paris' literary history. When I opened its thick pages, I realized they were not cut. I had to take a pair of scissors and cut the pages that were printed in folded sheets.

Now they sell repro posters of Janice Joplin, Marilyn Monroe and every book stall seems to have photos of Audrey Hepburn – more of an icon now than ever. I walk pass so many open-faced stalls of old and new books, tattered or pristine, until I get to the Pont Neuf and cross at the tip of lle de la cite where Notre Dame rests near the Square du Vert Gallant. This green square of land on the island tip provides an unobstructed view of the Seine. I feel as though I'm in the middle of this river riding along its currents and my vantage point is the bow of this little ship of land.

I try to breathe it all in, fix my gaze far and make my mind click like an old Polaroid camera. I'll keep this picture and its smells in my mind and heart. Paris makes you want to do that – to capture memories that will last through the cold harsh days of life when you need something warm and happy to fuel your spirit. Paris gives that gift.

I wander back over to Ile Saint Louis and walk across the river side where there are no bouquinnistes. No entrepreneurial book stalls are allowed - only apartments and homes for the wealthy. I walk on their front lawn, the Seine, and gaze down as the sun shines off its surface. I walk down steep steps to the lower banks of sidewalks and notice fat swans squatting in groups as though defending their little spot of Paris. Not too many strollers, just me but those who do pass smile as though we are the smart ones who just enjoy the now. I climb up another set of stairs that lead to another bridge to cross over. Even though the traffic light is with me, I cross very carefully. The right of pedestrians does not really exist in Paris.

On the other side of this main thoroughfare are side streets that meander through smaller fewer commercial areas. I stop at a cafe for a café crème – one of the many pleasures which I would never think of doing in the US. A small café with a friendly bonjour Madame and an impeccable small cup and saucer with frothy coffee and milk makes for a delicious pause in a delightful day.

The waiter and I exchange pleasantries – he is in fact the owner. The café had been his father's before him. He tells me his son goes to the Poly Tech as though I know what that means. In fact, I had read about it. It's the very prestigious school in Paris where Marie Curie and Louis Pasteur went. His voice his voice is full of pride.

"You must be very proud of him."

"Oui Madame, I am."

The French take pride in so many things - their culture, their language, and the importance of intellect. It is one of the few countries or the only country that has an Academy which oversees the use of the French language in journalism, advertising, television etc. The French know their syntax and grammar both in the written and spoken word. Through the years they have attempted to keep English out of the French language. Concessions have been made. The French have adapted, up to a point.

Try at conversation and you will be met more than halfway. F. Scott Fitzgerald said, "France has the only two things toward which we drift as we grow older – intelligence and good manners."

The French seem to have a pride in ownership. You see waiters and owners sweeping the side sidewalk in front of their establishment and hosing down the walkway before the morning coffee customers come. Can you imagine a worker in CVS washing the windows and sidewalk before customers arrive? Doubtful, it's not in his job description and if it were, he probably would not take the job.

Before I leave, I ask him if there is a bookstore near here. "Oui Madame, Shakespeare and Company is just over there". He leads me out of the café and points up the street –to the most famous bookstore in Paris. I recognize the area now.

It was the only English bookstore in Paris in the 1920's. Sylvia Beach established it on the Rue de l'Odeon. She helped many American writers including F. Scott Fitzgerald and Ernest Hemingway. Her store was a haven for British and American authors - T.S. Eliot, James Joyce and Ezra Pound all came under her wing, but during WWll she had to close the doors. 1940 saw the end of Shakespeare and Company until the 1950's when a man named George Whitman bought part of her inventory and borrowed the name to reestablish its prominence for English books on rue St Julien-le-Pauvre on the left bank across from Notre Dame. New and vintage books now line the shelves and no longer are the likes of Henry Miller, Ferlinghetti, and Dylan Thomas writing and talking in the early morning hours on the upper floor of Shakespeare and Company. Like a Chaucerian Inn George used to invite itinerant writers, professors, intellectuals, and students to sleep over in the writers' room above his store. How my life might have changed if I had done that. It would have been an adventure to remember in my old age. I dreamt of being a female Fitzgerald - who knows 'what might have been?'

Today when I visit, I look for familiar nooks and crannies- the chaotic tower of books and the French ones hidden under the staircase, but it has changed – The upper sanctum is reserved for speakers. Now there are announcements on the website for author signings etc. No impromptu invitations by the tall lanky angular George. A bon vivant, a literary legend of another time not Sylvia Beach's but a time when the likes of younger writers of the late fifties and sixties would enamor their audiences with pearls of wisdom. I talk to the young cashiers – perhaps unaware of the likes of these men maybe even of George himself who died a few years ago at the age of 98. A new generation of Shakespeare and Company devotees, who know the music but not the rhythm of other times crunch into the tiny archaic building. I hear some talk of their writing ability and what they desire and that writing in Paris is an incredible experience. I envy them their dreams, positivity, and assurance. And I also am happy that young people know and dream of this literary heritage that came from the post war generation of WW1 not the X or Y generation of the millenniums but the men who stayed on to recover their souls after the war to end all wars ended. We stand in line to participate in a writing seminar in the loft. A recent grad of some Midwestern university says he has taken time not to get a job but to come to Paris to write. A girl in front of him says,

"And how is that working out?"

"Not famous yet, but I'm working at it."

Come to Paris to write or if you decide to buy a book at George's store, it will be stamped with Shakespeare's head and encircled with Shakespeare and Co. Kilometer Zero Paris stamp. I bought a Colombo detective novel, pages on the left in English on the right in French. Peter Falk is on the cover. This iconic 1970's T.V. series was famous in America, but the book with its Shakespeare and Company logo and stamp is priceless since I bought it in Paris.

I walk around the corner to see another building, the Hotel Esmeralda, named after Victor Hugo's literary heroine Esmeralda in the Hunchback of Notre Dame. The hotel has existed since 1646 so it is not a five- star American hotel with suites etc. However, it is well worth your time to enter and see the staircase and charming lobby depicted in *Linnea's Garden,* a children's book about a little girl and her friend the Japanese gardener. The Swedish author of this children's book used the hotel for the setting. Linnea and her friend the Japanese gardener want to visit Monet's Garden. The book is about their visit to Giverny, Monet's home, but it is also about their stay in Paris in this hotel.

Across from the hotel is a little park next to Saint Julien le Pauvre, considered to be the oldest church in Paris, two years older than Notre Dame in 1165. Without a bell tower or ornate spires its simplicity and plain archaic edifice sets it apart from the busy Paris of the 21st century.

The church has been rebuilt twice since the 1100's. No fancy gardens, just a few rose bushes and flowering plants on the sandy soil that surround this small parcel of land. Weekends are busy with concerts with pianists and string combos in this small stone sanctuary. Performed at a modest price they convey the sound and beauty of another age.

Around the corner is a street full of cafes and restaurants with cheaper but not good French fast food , Greek gyros and even fat juicy hamburgers with greasy french fries at a place called Le Hamburger. The streets may be cobblestones but the shout outs from waiters to entice you into their restaurants is strictly New York bowery. I listen and say 'non, merci' and keep walking. Never turn to look back, push forward past the rabbits hanging in the windows near the plates of chicken legs and pig heads. I need something less exotic... and something well-cooked, solid French fare. Smells of garlic, tomatoes, and basil filter through the air.

I pass over an avenue, cross in front of Notre Dame and head for the Marais, the old Jewish district of Paris. This area of the 4th is very 'in': translation - chic and expensive I choose one quickly before they clean and set up for dinner. I pick the corner seat where I can people watch. A regular is to my right and the waiter greets her with the obligatory kisses which brush the side of the face – a real skill or else you lock noses simultaneously. He deals with the two women to my left in a formal but polite manner. When he brings their dessert, they say in faulty French that they did not order any. He nicely explains that it came with the lunch and is included. No condescending manner - just smoothly efficient and polite. To me he says. "The same?"

"What is the same ?"

"A salad with shrimp, carrots and tomatoes with camembert - and the plat principal [entrée] is quiche Lorraine."

The fresh shrimp and carrot and tomato salad arrive with a healthy slab of camembert, bread, and a glass of red wine. By the time the piping hot quiche arrives I am totally relaxed and making judgements in my mind about the shoes, red with straps across the toes or ankle ballet flats and military boots, passing by. All are memorable. Their owners seem to dance across the street and nimbly sidestep tourists on the sidewalk. The natives, the Parisians, wear short little jackets, slim cut pants or even beautifully tailored coats, too warm for not yet fall; the jackets and coats have lines of asymmetrical buttons and unusual lapels. The air of effortless chic abounds.

"Too warm," I hear a voice next to me whistle out as though reading my thoughts. And then, "red wine, Monsieur Jacques' the woman says to the waiter, "and a carafe of water, s'il vous plait". She mixes her English accent between French and English.

"Oui, Madame Benoit."

'It's hot,' she comments to me in English. "They never bring you any water. Where are you from my dear?" she says as she bends down to pat her pug nestled beneath her chair.

"The United States. How did you know?'

She glances down at my turquoise trail runners - sneakers by any other name.

"I've been admiring all the chic shoes in store windows and on French feet since 1968. I went from sandals to converse sneakers, to boots and now to wide rubber soled shoes that let me walk. I'm all about comfort at my age. When I think about it, my shoe wardrobe is accompanied by jeans, flowy shirts and skirts." She extends her hand. "Louise from London, once upon a time, now from Paris I'm part of all the other ex-pats who get to stay because they married French. I'm more French than British although I'm minus the husband now. Just my man Boris." She indicates the pug snorting under the bistro chair.

"Actually, he's more American than British or French. On hot days he must have his climatisee, air conditioning. My apartment has it. Summers here are infernos. The French evacuate in August and go to their second homes by the sea or ocean. The winters are really cold and grey, so Boris is dressed in his Burberry coat. Everyone in my neighborhood and the places I frequent adore him. He gets meat scraps from the boucherie, ham from the charcuterie, and bread from the boulangerie. Hence, he is not a slim Parisian."

She continues to tell me of her life in Paris for the last 50 years – the myths and the realities of living away from your home. I like Louise; she is direct. "I noticed you got the specialite du jour – so if you're on a budget like me and prefer to people watch rather than eat in Michelin star restaurants. I'm going to write down a list of go-to spots in Paris – all are free or cost but a pittance. Le bateau Moche and the Eiffel Tower are must sees and the ticket cost is worth it."

"Remember the tip is included in France so you can give an extra euro or so but not an extra 15 to 20 percent because you've already paid that in the bill."

I do not mention that I know this and some of her other advice. I appreciate that she reaches out to a stranger in her city. She places the bills she has counted out and leaves them under the check before she pushes up from the table. Come, you can help walk me home, and I'll show you two places to visit.

We meander in the sunlight with her iron grip around my arm. Her build is sturdy, but her legs and feet are not securely placed. We walk around a corner, and she pauses a bit to get her balance before continuing on past the Place des Vosges. We cut through the park, and she says I'm over here and waves her hand in the direction of some lovely old apartment buildings. La Place or park is in the middle of this square of mansion type apartments of another time when horse drawn carriages led people home to the gas lit square.

Louise interrupts my thoughts, "You go that way to see Victor Hugo's house and then the Musee Carnavalet. Both are free and so lovely.'

We bid goodbye the French way with side kisses but then she takes my hand in a firm American handshake. I follow the way she indicates under the arched passageways that surround the square. The once old homes house shops. The front windows beam with artfully decorated 'must-haves'. I peak behind an open gate and see a millinery shop – ribbons, hats with plumes and feathers fancy enough for the Ascot races. I'd like Louise's commentary on this place. What was it in the 1860's or 1960's? Now it's full of ribbons and sewing supplies. I think it's interesting that this tiny tucked away shop can survive in this expensive area of art, designer fashion and jewelry boutiques.

Old and young women, dressed in jeans or in Channel, have bags of buttons in their hands and swaths of ribbons tangling from their arms. They 'pardonnez-excusez' yet push ahead. The British queue up; Americans mill around; and the French just politely say excuse me and push. Me, I sneak to the side and check out the tag on a bolt of modern white fabric with green and tangerine abstract lines. The sticker tag shocks me. The shop might seem antiquated and shabby, but it is shabby chic – Hampton style, with prices to match. The messy semi dirty fabric stores on the lower streets below Sacre Coeur had some high prices but not as steep as these. There I had bought a remnant of navy and white abstract print for a foulard and a few meters of navy, gray and white abstract linen for a simple of so chic dress. So, when I wear the scarf or the dress, I'll think of Montmartre. But I am not buying here for memories of the Marais and the beautiful park. I can keep the memories without the high price fabric. Either these French women are creative wizards at making haute couture or they have seamstresses or decorators expertly tailoring pieces for them.

I walk out and over to an archway that leads to the Hotel Sully, as I pass, I see a sign for Victor Hugo's home. I take a right and I am in his old apartment, one of the many he used but never owned. Dark and ornately decorated in the style of the 19th century, the luxury of the wood, wall papered walls and floors show a man who enjoyed design. His home reflects his writing style, sentences embellished with words like so many jewels in a crown. All nationalities come to view where the great author lived, but only his many porcelain Chinese dog dragons, sitting on the dark wood bookshelves and on the floor stare back.

I feel the oppressive nature of the house. It matches his dark and gloomy novels. He was a stone's throw from Notre Dame and his famous 'Hunchback'. There is no view of the mighty church since his secluded rooms look inward onto the beautiful square. No natural light spreads through the rooms.

One window, oval almost like a ship portal looks out over the park, enclosed with trees, and surrounded by red rose building facades. This window looks over the delightful square and a tall pair of glass French doors opens onto a tiny balcony, barely a barrier from a fall from the window ledge. All the building windows have this accessory. Perhaps on a sunny day light enters this somber room. Now children's slides, swings, and bicycles chained to the iron fence are the view. Young people come and sit here to talk, eat, and laugh while children play with their grandmothers or mothers – probably the same existed in Victor Hugo's time. I wonder if he wrote facing the park or sat in a dark corner.

$\mathcal{D}ay$ 10

SEPTEMBER 28

"Twenty years from now you will be more disappointed by the things that you didn't do than the ones you did do. So, throw off the bowlines. Sail away from the safe harbor. Catch the trade winds in your sail. Explore, Dream, Discover."

MARK TWAIN

Part of this thirty-day journey is to rediscover my independence. When we are young, we travel or try new things with few expectations or concerns. As we grow up, we pick, choose, and eliminate places and events before we even go. As women travelers we need to cast off from our moorings, lift our sails, and slide out into the waters of life – they may be calm, choppy, or turbulent, but we won't know until we try.

I have mastered the metro, the subway transportation system, and have become more confident. I take different metro lines at various times every day. I must confess I do not take them at night. As a woman alone, I feel more vulnerable, so I usually have an early dinner rather like those Florida snowbirds who always get the early bird special (but that does not exist here). Afterwards I choose to leisurely walk- along the Seine - back to my flat. There I read or write in my journal about my day. I think about what I have seen or what I will see tomorrow. I might watch and try to understand French T.V., take the time to skype, what's app friends and family or just sit out in my garden and look out up at the Paris sky.

Because I am in my own silent environment, I enjoy the human contact on the metro. Encounters are few, yet people are people and I enjoy watching them. Often on the trains a musician/singer hops on board a car to give a rendition of a familiar tune. At the end he asks for a donation with his hand or his hat. One man begins singing a popular Charles Trenet song which was not bad, but then he switches to 'Oh, Champs Elysees" a song that American students sing in French classes. Many smirk –many because of the song, or because he is singing it flat. The blond middle-aged woman next to me takes out a book to read – a ploy that riders use to isolate themselves. Under her breath she murmurs, 'It's too early in the morning for this."

This day I'm going to Pere Lachaise, the famous cemetery in the 20th arrondissement. It will take three different metro lines. I might have to endure many singers, but it will be worth it. 'Pere Lachaise,' Paris's most well-renown cemetery is high up on a hill in the city's eastern corner, the 20th arrondissement. The land once owned by Father Lachaise, confessor to King Louis XIV, was sold to Napoleon in order to provide a new cemetery. He did not foresee all the notables who would be buried there or even conceive that an American singer would find his way among the elite.

An uphill walk from the last metro stop I manage to find the entrance gate and the detailed maps in a holding box which indicate the street names of the cemetery and the names of the famous writers, composers, singers, artists, and actors buried here. The American, Jim Morrison- lead singer of the Doors, is somehow buried here because he died in Paris. His tomb is a mecca for old hippies or new age hippies or simply curiosity seekers. I pass by it just to see the strewn pipes, red roses, wine, and Jack Daniels bottles. Park cleanup crews clear the stuff out daily but by the next morning new pagan entities line his grave.

The stones, the tombs, the paths are all very Edgar Allen Poe like; I expect some crazed raven to swoop down despite the sunlight. No one to talk to but the dead, yet there's a presence even among the ones whose names are illegible. All that stone and ceremony is erased over time. No one to remember or to know whoever was there. Tourists come to see the 'greats' – the history of France in a small plot of land, but this is not a walk for the chic heel types. Me, I walk for two hours over cobble stoned streets and stone paths to find a few of 'my' memorable ones – Yves Montand, singer, actor, and husband to Simone Signoret. His song ' Il n'y a plus d'apres' is about two lovers who meet years later in a café in Saint Germain des Pres. Montand and Signoret had a tumultuous relationship through other love affairs and tragedies, but in the end the great love and history they had together linked the two of them together for all eternity side by side in Pere Lachaise.

Then of course I must find another singer of France and of Paris, Edith Piaf. I find her grave unimposing and tragic like her life. A small marker with her only living child's name, Marcelle, who died at age two lies adjacent to hers. Her last husband, twenty years younger than she, died not too long after her in 1971 and is buried alongside. Her grave reflects the two Piaf songs I love the most: 'La Vie en Rose' and 'Je ne regrette rien'. I am not like Edith I do have regrets. The main one is that I did not spend my youth in Paris. If I had, perhaps I would have had a 'rose colored life'.

I visit Honoré de Balzac, Eugene de la Croix, Alice B. Toklas of marijuana brownie fame and Gertrude Stein, her lover who was writer and a mentor to Hemingway. I give up on finding Marcel Proust, Oscar Wilde, and Frederic Chopin. I have had enough of the crushing stones, the tumbling monuments, and the trees with arms too long. I leave. I have spent enough time spent figuring out when they died and matching their years to mine. I have time – certainly, to live and not wander among the dead.

We are so concerned about our neighbors when we are alive, but do we actually give any thought to who we will share our 'earth' plots with for all eternity? I was glad to join the lively metro crowds. On the way back an "in your face' duo who sang along with their boom box, a relic from the 1980's. They blocked the train door as they got in. They danced as well as sang and encouraged anyone who was near them to join in. I did not mind after spending time too quiet a time with the dead. Of course, I was at the end of the car far from their incoherent loud and fast French rap. Then as unceremoniously as they arrived, they left. The car breathed a sigh of relief.

Onward to fun – from the dead paths to the most vibrant avenue in the world – Avenue des Champs Elysees where the famous – Marlena Dietrich, Duchess of Windsor and the not so famous used to live. Now it is an avenue of history and mega shopping. Near the end of the Champs Elysees is another free museum Louise recommended 'le Petit Palais. – filled with 'crapauds', toads, which makes me smile.

This wide avenue begins at La Place de la Concord and extends to L'Etoile (the star) under the Arc de Triomphe where 11 other avenues meet, encircling the Arc that Napoleon had begun in 1806 and not finished until 1836 after his downfall. Here the Tomb of the Unknown Soldier was buried in 1920 after WW1. He lies in rest under the Arc.

Les Champs Elysees, bordered by chestnut trees and sidewalks on either side, was and is a place to promenade. Horse drawn carriages would let ladies out in their wide skirts, expansive coats, and hats with veil and plumes. Men dressed in long waist coats, dress trousers and top hats would accompany them down the Avenue. Carriages were replaced by cars and then tanks which desecrated the landscape from 1940-1944. After the

Liberation of Paris triumphal processions flourished, the Avenue was returned to flaneurs, bicycles, motorcycles, and cars. I walk as far as the Louis Vuitton building, constructed like a large leather suitcase. It makes me realize that Paris is the fashion capital of the world and to walk down Les Champs Elysees in sneakers and sweats would be sacrilege. Although I am not dressed like that, my attire does not register on the chic scale today. I turn back toward the metro Clemenceau Champs Elysees to get my bearings.

Le Petit Palais and the frogs and toads are my goal. To get there I pass formal gardens laid out in 1838 and used as part of the World Fair in 1855. I cut across to le Petit Palais, a charming building, with steps that curve gracefully up from the street. Le Petit Palais is like a mini palace and was created for another exhibit in 1900. Today, despite the security check points and entrance counter, I still feel like I'm entering a ballroom. It houses mainly 19th century painters, including many of the impressionists. I pass by the Mary Cassatt paintings and rooms of ornate cabinets and chairs.

A large vase is in the center of the entry area, and I ask a British couple to take my photo. I feel happy in the sunlight shining through the glass windows and roof of this gem of a building. We chat and they tell me about the 'tea' area in the back of the museum. I take their advice and go to sit at a little table among artists sketching and people writing in journals in this oasis of greenery. High green willows, a bubbling fountain, and muted flowers flourish in the center of this space. The café offers coffee and croissants; I opt for that and sit in my pleasant solitude drinking in the light and the sun and marveling at how lucky I am to be here in such a serene haven.

Refreshed, I wander through the clean, sunlit, eclectic rooms. The variety of art and of people is astounding. All nationalities, including the French with their children, look carefully at the art. A tripod with a parasol and easel is set up in a room. A reproduction painting of the artist Ernest - Jules Renoux 1863-1932 is set up on the easel with a vintage artist paint box filled with tins and paint tubes.

A little curly dark-haired boy peers into the box and then looks very closely at the painting. He seems mesmerized by the colors and the arrangement of the tubes of paint and brushes placed in orderly rows in the case.

His father wags a finger, and the boy does not touch. I find such simple action fascinating and wonder what the future will hold for this child. Will he become a painter, baker, politician, government worker, or just a man doing an everyday job and appreciating the culture and beauty surrounding him?

I move on to stand in front of large fat' crapauds' (toads) and grenouilles' (frogs), made by Jean Carries in the 1800's. I am delighted by their texture, form, and color. If I had a traveling companion, he/she would not want to spend so much time looking at these unattractive creatures. Yet Paris has attractions for every interest and type of person, and soon the crapauds and grenouilles have another admirer. The little boy  pulls on his father's jacket and points to the toads. He touches one and then another totally, enthralled with each one's uniqueness. I marvel how children can find such joy in the everyday things of life. They live in the moment and then pass into the next one.

Reluctantly, I leave. I cannot stay in Tolkien land forever. I move on - to the art deco room of furniture with artfully crafted pear wood walls.

Day 11

SEPTEMBER 29

"The real voyage of discovery consists not in seeking new landscapes but in having new eyes."

- MARCEL PROUST

Each day before I leave, I reread the quotes I wrote down before I began my trip to Paris. I want some inspirational ideas that will prod and push me out every day to seek new adventures. Today the Paris sky has turned its formidable gray – not like shiny zinc but the gray of a well-worn garden tool or the iron grating at the Gare Saint Lazare. My eyes glance up to the sky above my little garden studio. The eternal question arises – umbrella or no umbrella? I look at the basket of wet laundry I need to carry and answer no.

This green garden studio advertised a washing machine, and I stupidly assumed there would be a dryer because after all what good is a pile of wet sheets and towels. My purpose today is to dry the clothes that took six hours to wash last night. I checked the machine every hour on the hour and still it was not finished. Redesigning them into fantastic haute couture, a Halston Grecian draped dress, I thought. After hours of washing, rinsing, draining, and spinning they were clean but wet. With no or low expectations, I enter the seven day per week laundromat I had spotted on the corner going to and from the metro. Not exactly how I want to spend my day in Paris, but it is 'new landscape' and I'll have to look at it with 'new eyes' and determination if I want clean sheets and clothes. I could have called the host of my apartment, but she seems too dippy. I got a hold of her somehow after the internet went down. She blithely said she was late with her payment. Yes, they disconnect in every country if you do not pay your bill. I did not want to have a similar conversation, so I took on a new adventure.

Maybe the laundromat would provide a new experience in Paris – from the mundane to the marvelous. When I had passed the laundromat before I had seen no one. Today six men are inside. I enter. The oldest opens the door. I hear English with a Scottish burr. The oldest, the Scotsman, is speaking to a group of three. The youngest, an Adam Levine type, thin and tattooed up one arm and down the other, pushes his wire rimmed glasses up as he listens. The others stand by the dryers and are conversing in French. I nod and say hello and put my clothes in two dryers. I ask the two Frenchman how to use the dryer. One would think you would put in euros like we do quarters - but no. First, I must buy tokens, then are put in the machines.

Adam Levine sees I have success and asks, "How do the machines work?"

"Not too hard." I show him the ropes. He too has an apartment nearby with no washer, no dryer, and no instructions about where or how to use the laundromat. So, the landscape of the laundromat has changed. It is French and therefore somewhat exotic to me. It is a mundane but not an odious task. Adam Levine and I chat on this overcast day.

His name, of course, is not Adam Levine but he is a singer, Gary Jules. Paired up with a French singer in a duet combo for a concert tour, he finished his show at the Bercy Stadium. Crazy how serendipity works. I am renting on a street named Saint Sebastian, my grandson's name, and this man's last name is my Sebastian's middle name, Sebastian Jule. Gary

Jules was born in La Jolla California where I spent some of my childhood. His sister is a writer, like me, and lives in Boulder where I was interested in moving to. One of his favorite spots is Pere La Chaise – maybe he's a Jim Morrison fan. I don't ask. When I talked to my son that night, he tells me Gary Jules sings "Tears for Fears". I know the song. What I didn't know was that Gary Jules is one of his favorite singers.

Maybe he will write a song about Pere la Chaise. He says that he stays in this section, the 11th, when he comes to sing at the famous Bercy in the 13th. His wife and two children have come. I like how so many wives and husbands include the whole family in their job schedules. I always had to do it all myself. I should have gone out on my own a long time ago. If my ex could not change to accommodate us, then I should have made the change before so many years passed, but people are reluctant to change-even if they are in a bad place. The steps to altering it involve too much effort, thought, and money. So often others make the change for us whether we want it or not. Perhaps boyfriends, husbands, exes or even children give us advice – make changes for us - acting as though they know what is best for us. We women need to initiate change. "No one puts baby in the corner" should be our motto. Act before someone puts you there.

Even total strangers try to make up our minds about minor or major decision. For example, a taxi driver told me I must go to the Moulin Rouge. Going to a revue of mostly naked women is not my idea of optimum entertainment. The allure is lost on me... unless I aspire to be a nude stage performer. That job is for a twenty-year-old or Jennifer Lopez. No exercise regime in the world is going to get me a body like hers.

I also ignored his advice because le Moulin Rouge is just up from Pigalle - not the best neighborhood- unless you don't mind waiting under a streetlight for a taxi, but who knows what other kind of car might stop by. I feel safer walking during the day and seeing other types of entertainment.

Laundry dropped off - boulevards to cross, the bells of Notre Dame beckon. I hear them, their 850th anniversary. Crowds are lined up under the gray sky. It is a good day to go underground beneath the Ile de la Cite to a museum of archeological treasures. Old stones and walls from pre-roman times encircle the banks of the underground Seine. The tip of the island used to extend about thirty yards into the river. It was deep enough for a port. I try to imagine the lifestyle that existed more than a thousand years ago. The artifacts in these underground passageways portray a hard life, a life of bare necessities and definite scarcity.

Enough of breathing in the dusty air of the past, I climb up the stairs into the air and today's more luxurious life. I head for the Musee des Arts Decoratifs on Rue de Rivoli. located in the 1ˢᵗ arrondissement in the Louvre's western wing. It houses ceramics, glassware, and furniture from the Middle Ages up to the present. Floors exhibit furniture in various decades; the 1930's and 40's are my favorites. I adore the leopard chairs and the snakeskin settees. I pass by midcentury modern, AKA 1950's. In my mind that was not a desirable decade; I watched tv on those couches and put my Welsh's milk jar on the tables. My mother would tell me not to make rings on the tables. Going up and down all the stairs and not being allowed to sit on this furniture makes me tired and hungry. No need to check with anyone, I head off to find a restaurant.

Off of the Rue Rivoli is Saint Honoré and la Galerie Vero-Dodo, a passageway created in the 1700's. Like an early version of our malls yet more spectacular, its blue and white stone floors and the glass ceiling that looks to the light highlights old shops which now serve as stores but by appointment only. They seem like a stage set, and I expect characters to enter and begin conversing with one another. Above the Dickens like fronts and doors are small windows where shop owners used to live.

I follow a delicious aroma to a restaurant, 19 Galerie Vero-Dodo. I peer inside –not many people. A waiter notices my uncertainty.

"Madame, sit here." He says as he takes his towel from his shoulder and sweeps it over the chair. My table is outside as though on display like the windows surrounding me. People pass and look. I am amazed at such a chic and quiet oasis.

Without even asking, he brings me a glass and a carafe of red wine. Ceremoniously, he pours it into my glass. Then he brings water and a menu. "I recommend le plat du jour"… "Sounds perfect."

I do not mind sitting here like a mannequin on display. I enjoy being in the moment. I people watch and they watch me. I take a page from my son's playbook and discretely use my phone to take a shot of my lunch, a delightful creamy mussel soup and for the 'plat', salted lamb perfectly arranged with petit carrots and parsnips in an out-of-this world sauce. I am not blogging or putting moment by moment details on Facebook. I'm relaxing and eating a fine meal. What's not to enjoy? The piece de resistance for me is always the dessert. The crème-brulé is extraordinary. I crack the crust with the perfect dessert spoon and savor the cream beneath the crackling sugar surface. Most of the time, I think I should just order dessert and forget the meal, but in this case, I'm glad I ordered both. The best in life is often the simplest - the moments you don't plan but just stumble upon.

Walking back past my favorite square, Leopold Achille, in the 3rd arrondissement I enter through its black gate and sit on a bench facing the sand path and green lawn in the middle. Above is the building with the three large arched windows which look across this little park to the faded distressed rose- colored apartments on the other side. Tall green wide leaf plants and smaller yellow flowered ones grow in front of the iron fences separating the square from the road. How wonderful, I think to live in one of these apartments and look over the square and come out and sit in the sun like a big orange cat as I age. Colette, the writer, did just that but she was in the affluent Place Royale and wrote at her desk looking over luxurious gardens. Paris speaks to every woman in her own way.

No longer having the bladder of a camel, I'm always on the lookout for les toilettes. I know the Musee Carnavalet has them. I cross into the heart of the Marais in the 4th and to museum that holds a new favorite artist, the Japanese artist of the 50's Leonard Foujita. I adore his 'Hotel Edgar Quinet Boulevard EQ'. The front of the hotel is like a sepia photograph. It faces a street with somber bare trees lining a grey sidewalk. Sparse brushstrokes indicate a walker with his dog in the foreground and a background of roofs and coal stacks against the slate-colored Paris sky. Another painting that I love shows the interior of a bistro. In the foreground are chairs and tables where people sit, talk, or write, and behind is a zinc bar counter with a wall of wine bottles and a bartender. It's a typical bistro, a place for the beat generation of the times, in the Latin Quarter, 1958. Such spots also existed in New York and San Francisco.

Besides bistros, museums are wonderful places to be alone yet with people. It's personal to decide to stand or sit to view a painting. I enter another world and imagine the people in the painting with their lives of joys and sorrows. I wonder how difficult or easy it was for them to live in those times. I wonder if the artist made a living from his or her, paintings?

"Do you know he was Japanese, Madame?" A voice cuts through my thoughts. I had not seen the man in the dark blue uniform when I entered.

"You must enjoy seeing this every day. Rather like your own painting?"

'Oui, that is exactly how I feel." He begins to tell me about Leonard Tsuguharu Foujita who was born and schooled in Tokyo but came to study art in Paris. "He lived here from 1910 through the 1920's. He was one of the most influential artists of the twentieth century. His studio was in Montparnasse, and he stayed here for many years before traveling to the south of France and then to Argentina."

"Did he know Picasso?'

"Yes, and you must visit that museum when you return. It's under renovation now."

I like how he assumes I will return.

"Foujita died in 1968 the year of our third revolution. We had Victor Hugo's Les Misérables in 1846 then the students of May 1968 which brought the government to a standstill. Ah, I remember it well."

"You sound like Maurice Chevalier," I laugh.

"Oui madame, but you can't possibly remember him?"

I smile. The French are so gallant about a woman's age.

"I know his movie *Gigi* very well." I do not tell him how many times I watched it as a girl – too much information.

We continue to talk, and he tells me that the museum is closing soon, but of course, "You can come back tomorrow to view your painting."

I can't afford that Foujita painting or any of his unless I lived in the 1920's when he was first beginning, but I will get a special reminder of this day. As I walk, I hear the song "Putting on the Ritz". I start tapping my foot and merge into the crowd on Rue des Francs Bourgeois. An elderly woman in a flapper dress with lavender fringe and a pink cloche hat is dancing in the street to a cello, saxophone, clarinet, and trombone combo. I thought about Foujita maybe he would have been in a café in Montparnasse listening to this song or walking pass Zelda Fitzgerald in Saint Germain des Pres.

The music brings a beautiful fragrance. It emanates from an open shop door, Claudalie, across the way. Within half an hour the salesman has sold me a beautiful bag of l'eau de toilette, hand cream, and body lotion, all made from the residue of the wine process. Whenever I put it on, I'll think about my Paris escape in the museum Carnavalet with a Japanese painter called Foujita and the heady times of the 1920's.

$\mathcal{D}ay$ 12/13

SEPTEMBER 30/ OCTOBER 1

To my mind, the greatest reward of travel is to be able to experience everyday things as if for the first time, to be in a position in which almost nothing is so familiar that it is taken for granted."

BILL BRYSON

The word for today is chocolate one of my most favorite foods; in fact, my three basic food groups are chocolate, bread, and cheese. Wine as the beverage of choice. I could eat these every day. None of them are healthy so I am forced to eat in moderation. However, there was a woman – French, of course, who at age 105 decided to change her dietary habit to only one glass of red wine, one cigarette, and two pieces of chocolate a day. She continued along with her 'normal' French cuisine. That was her version of moderation a la vie de Benjamin Franklin. It was said she lived to be 122.

Today brings two tours: one is of the Garnier Opera House in the 9th and a chocolate tour of five chocolate shops all within walking distance of one another in the 7th. My younger daughter booked the Phantom Tour which is what she called it since the Garnier Paris Opera is where the phantom of the Opera story began. The beauty of these tours is that you can go online and see what interests you; look at the price, times, distance from one's abode and book it. The instructions and ticket number are emailed to you.

After my son-in-law booked the bread and croissant tour which I loved so much, my daughter booked two more. It is a memorable gift to see something you have never seen before. These two outings fit the bill for my birthday. I had seen Phantom of the Opera in New York and had the reference of the stage set before I walked into the Palais Garnier, but even that could not prepare me for the wide winding staircase, the golden ornate loges, and the chandeliers. I half expected to see ladies in rustling silks and delicate lace with dresses caressing the steps of the staircase of the Opera Garnier.

Garnier's first and last work paid homage to Napoleon 111. It was barely finished when the Franco Prussia war broke out and siphoned all the money out of France's treasury. Our guide explains this to us as she takes us through the halls and seats of the theatre. Sitting in the orchestra, we look up at the ceiling of angels, cherubs, and flowers. Renovated in the early 1900's by Marc Chagall, it is a mini museum of his paintings all in one spot. The guide's constant stream of facts and stories brings the theater to life, and I can imagine the water beneath the stage and the boats that the phantom used in the below ground moats. The phantom even had his own loge, number 5. We all take selfies in front of that door. I was going for a chic look in my mustard and gray sweater with an intelligent owl, not a crazy QVC sequined one on the front. Muted and fashionable beneath a fitted black leather jacket, the owl was the perfect choice. It said understated, smart, and Parisian. If the phantom walked out, he would notice.

The following day is the chocolate tour. We meet close by in the Marais. We are a group of mostly women in our thirty's through 70's , dressed in a variety of attire. Some wear jeans that look incredible – with just enough slouch to carry off a white pressed shirt and dangling bohemian earrings. One woman courageously wears brown loafers with no socks – very 1960's. Looks great now – hope she can finish the walk without too many blisters. Another stand- out gal has perfectly coiffured hair – a blond bob with streaks that no natural sun could account for. Her face is made up with perfect foundation, blush, and powder. She reminds me of a more robust Catherine Deneuve. Her attire is head to toe, camel brown - a pencil skirt with matching princess heels and a twin set (a sweater and cardigan) in the same matching camel color. Her nails are bright red to match her lipstick and she wears gold accessories, a thick gold chain around her beginning to crease neck – probably bought in Italy – the gold chain not the neck and big round gold earrings along with a bracelet chain to finish off the look. Her fashion accessory guru must be Iris Apfel. "Don't take one item off just add two more."

As we enter each shop, she focuses on every chocolate in their meticulous rows and on the words of the guide who explains the type of chocolate with its legal amount of cocoa bean percentage and its history. Then the guide puts a few on a Limoges plate and we pass it around. Catherine Deneuve nibbles her piece like a giant rabbit; I take two bites and mine is gone. We go to four consecutive chocolatiers and are given an exquisite piece of dark chocolate, only dark. I eat all of mine. The plump Catherine folds hers up in tissues and places them in her gold Versace bag.

"They're just too rich you know." She leans into her husband's camel sports coat." So rich I can't possibly eat them."

My motto is it's never too rich. Desserts and candy are meant to be eaten and never saved for another day. I used to hide my candy in secret places or freeze it so I would not gobble it all up. Perhaps it was in the summer that one of my children found a large gray no longer chocolate colored Easter bunny in the grandfather clock. I told them the Easter bunny must have been forgetful.

If you are going to order and place it on your plate, then you must eat it all. Face the facts, you're just going to crave it an hour later. Don't let it languish in the sun...or in your pocketbook when it can be in your stomach. And really, I think Catherine has not forgone much. Her spandex cannot conceal the extra pounds pulling her skirt tight across her midsection and hips. So why the pretext? If you choose a chocolate tour, then eat the chocolate! Our last stop to quench our thirst from all the chocolate is a shop that sells hot chocolate of course. It's so frothy that the spoon can practically stand up in the cream itself.

"Mesdames and Messieurs, I must tell you again that the cocoa beans have to be a certain percentage in France in the making of the chocolate.

The chocolatiers cannot dilute it and add more sugar and artificial additives for the same result. It must be pure." So much for Hersey bars.

I think she should have told us how much a person can consume to avoid toxicity from coco beans. I feel a migraine coming on from all of this. It's rather like eating a giant bag of M&M's in front of the T.V. on a Saturday night in one's pj's. Perhaps La grande Catherine had the right idea of moderation. I should refer to her as *Big Ben: "Everything in moderation."*

"Is the tour over now, mademoiselle?" a thin woman in a Lulu lemon black yoga outfit says. "I told a taxi to pick me up at this corner."

"Yes, if you wish. We are just walking back through the Marais."

Nice to be picked up by taxi throughout Paris. Perhaps this East Hampton type has scheduled in a yoga session or barre class to counter all the chocolate- 'chacun a son gout' each to one's taste as the French say.

We all seem to go our separate ways after the taxi woman leaves. Little camaraderie on this tour. Perhaps I just need a friend who knows all the inside jokes and can finish my sentences. Then again, I'll tell my friends when I return. We'll laugh then. I see the steeple and buttresses of Notre Dame in the distance and decide to cross over to the Seine and walk by the riverbank. The day is warm, and my head is feeling the pain of all that chocolate. It's beginning behind my left eye and at the back of my neck. Swimming and cold water would help, but I can't possibly swim in the Seine. Too murky to be appealing. I stop at one or two book seller stands on the sidewalk.

"May I help you, Madame? »

"Any Hemingway novels?"

"The American writer? – non"

I know they don't have any Hemingway novels – certainly not old ones. If I could find an English or French version from 1925; it would be worth thousands- enough for many return trips. I enjoy meandering and looking through old and new books, posters, and magazines. Marilyn Monroe and Audrey Hepburn, opposite icons, are in each stall. Again, one buys each to her own taste.

A little crepe stand that sells cold bottled water. The 4 euros for the small bottle of water is worth it. I press it on the back of my neck and the cold soothes the pain for a while. I pass between a break in the line of book stalls and walk down the steps near Pont de la Tournelle to walk along the wide roadway by the Seine.

A little boy, surfing the sidewalk, is pulling a skateboard with his dog on board. Joggers, cyclists, walkers, alone or hand in hand pass. All are enjoying the afternoon. So much to see and do, but then it's just the simple daily acts of living life that are so enjoyable, and the French seem to just do.

$\mathcal{D}ay$ 14

OCTOBER 2

"Stop worrying about the potholes in the road and celebrate the journey."

FITZHUGH MULLAN

Even when you are in the most fabulous city in the world, you can't stop totally thinking of your 'other life' because after all this is a vacation not a change of lifestyle. You think of what is happening in your 'other/normal life' while you are here? Focus on the journey. Live in the moment and brush those concerns aside.

My journey today is to see the Invalides, only two metro lines away - eight then thirteen. I conserve my walking to around 8 to 10 miles a day. Without a Fitbit I am from the school of estimation. I try to avoid aching feet and sore calves by getting to my destination of the day and spending the time walking around and appreciating the spot rather than getting lost trying to find it.

Les Invalides in the 7th district houses the remains of Napoleon Bonaparte beneath its gold-plated cupola that can be seen for miles. It is a complex of buildings: museums, monuments, a hospital, a church, and a retirement home for war veterans. The day is another sunny one and the walk across the green manicured lawns with bordering gardens is pleasurable. The sand paths lead to many buildings. I could spend an entire day here, but four hours immersed in war is all I can take. One can't worry about the potholes in the road when one sees the whole road blown up before you. To see and hear what soldiers endured in the name of war is incomprehensible. To view it through the perspective of Western times when most had the benefit of a life with a plan and choices is not possible, for in those times, to be fed and to feed one's children was not a given. The numbers who died and the dates have to be digested slowly. Inside the mausoleum is Napoleon's mahogany casket. He reigned as the supreme military tactician of canons and cavalry. The sun outside burns brightly and glistens through the glass, but the beauty does not make the slaughter any more palatable despite his fame.

All nationalities walk these grounds and corridors. I walk with them and hear Spanish, Italian, German, French, Hindu, Urdu, and English. Why do we come? To learn about this madness, this all-consuming need to go to war. Today there is a large contingency of old soldiers in uniforms with metals lined up on their chests. Half slung red berets cover bald heads or thinning hair – perhaps these soldiers in their seventies and eighties – are from the Algerian war or Vietnam, and those few in their nineties must be WWll Vets. They parade down a corridor. We outsiders watch.

I would have liked to hear their stories, but they are French and with their families. I look at all the war footage movies and encased weaponry, sacks, and uniforms behind glass displays. How did my father and father-in-law live from day to day or even hour to hour in the 'World' Wars. Their problems were mines in the road not potholes. Enough of the 'war' place, I walk to see Rodin, the sculptor.

A stone's, not a grenade's, throw from les Invalides is the Rodin Museum on Rue de Varenne. A copy of his thinker rests in the garden along with several other statues. The Kiss and The Gates of Hell are also housed here in the Hotel Biron which he used as a workshop from 1908 until his death in 1917. He decided to give all of his works plus paintings by Vincent Van Gogh, Paul Auguste Renoir, and Claude Monet to the French State if after his death, they would use the building to house his works. Established in 1919, Le Musee Rodin does just that and there is a room of Camille Claudel's work. Only after his death was his lover's works acknowledged in such a manner.

I pass this sunny day walking through the elaborate gardens and enjoying the roses still in bloom. Clusters and single benches rest among the statues and roses. I choose a stone bench in front of a statue of Victor Hugo and imagine what a conversation about the Hunchback of Notre Dame would be like. Afterwards I get an expresso in the inside café.

I do not feel like walking from the 7th to the 11th, so I break my rule and hop on the Varenne metro stop since it is so close. I'll walk from Hotel de Ville to my garden studio and perhaps catch the sunset this sunny October day, but before I return, I'll catch the exhibit about the resistance and Charles de Gaulle at the Hotel de Ville. Walking around and around it, I spot what I think is the entrance. A man is on duty at the door.

"Is there an exhibit about Charles de Gaulle concerning the resistance and WWll? "

I talk a bit about this interesting subject.

"Oui Madame, I know my history" Monsieur Smug answers.

I stumble on. "It was here in April. Is it still here?"

"You must ask at the entrance." All this he says with a Gaelic shrug and blasé expression.

Perhaps he knew his history, but he did not even know what was happening at the place that paid him to work. He reminded me of Kevin Kline in the Movie French Kiss. He had every mannerism including smoking a cigarette between his thumb and his forefinger. So arrogant.

"And the entrance is where, you idiot?" I say, but I leave off the 'idiot'.

Another stupid question. He just waves his arm off to the side in some general random direction.

Far from debonair or charming, some French are like oysters with little grains of sand stuck in their shells which do not form pearls of wisdom or charm just grains of annoyance. He probably knows how many potholes are on his street that the city of Paris must fix.

$\mathcal{D}ay$ 15

OCTOBER 3

"Every Exit is an entry somewhere else."

TOM STOPPARD

This line reminds me of Jean-Paul Sartre's play No Exit , performed in 1944 in Paris during the German Occupation. It begins with one man and two women trapped in a room with no exits. The audience learns that they must live in constant friction and animosity for eternity, and that eternity is in Hell. Sartre was a famous philosopher and writer, who along with his lifelong companion, Simone de Beauvoir, lived the existential life. One of her books, *The Second Sex*, advanced the cause and rights of women well before Gloria Steinem. Young women and girls today do not realize the rights and opportunities they have are because of such women who cleared the path.

To be/to exist rather than just to think was their philosophy. It resonated with me when I was young. Now it is more relevant than ever. I find myself trying to act rather than just talk about what I would like to do. I need to be of the Niki mindset - 'Just do it!'

Today, I am on my way to Sartre and Beauvoir's haunts in St Germain des Pres. As I exit line 4 near Place Sartre – Beauvoir, I look for signs to the De la Croix Museum which is small and out of the way. I decide that an early morning viewing is the best before any crowds. Of course, I cannot find it right away and meander down street after street. Early morning street sweepers are watering down the street on Rue Cardinal and a place called Place de la Furstenberg when I spot the museum entrance in the corner of quaint buildings tucked under shade trees.

I hear the bells of Saint Germain des Pres ringing on this cool overcast October morning. The roses are still blooming, and I think how lucky I am to have this solitude, but it comes with a price – a bit of loneliness. I want to see my grandson, Sebastian, running and playing in the Musee De la Croix's jewel of garden and his mother, breathing in the Paris air, with an expresso hand. She deserves a break to renew her spirits, and my son and daughter-in-law need to mend their hearts. Paris would provide the remedy.

I just sit here on a bench looking across the square to a building on the opposite side. I think of the tenants looking down on the flowers and paths of the museum Delacroix. Inside I walk the rooms of this house and drink in his paintings and sketches. He led the school of Romanticism with objectivity, color, and movement in his work. He lived primarily in the 1800's before the impressionist movement began in Paris. I become dizzy looking at the sketches and lithographs. The exactness and the details are astonishing, but I realize for all my love of art and seeing new things I have a saturation point, two to three hours inside is my limit. I attempt to read, look, understand, and remember. It takes too much mental concentration so like Sartre I must act; I leave.

No philosophical treatise or painting of a canvas just the act of finding a memorable place to eat, Le Flore or Les Deux Magots, is my goal. My 'raison etre' is to feel the presence of these two great writers. I follow the notes of a sweet saxophone around the corner of the church of Saint Germain des-Pres. I hear "I can't give you anything but love baby" and see a group, base, banjo, trumpet, and sax players, swinging harmoniously on the corner. Across the street is Café de Flore or simply le Flore of Jean-Paul Sartre's time. The white awning and green lettering are remnants of springtime no matter what the weather. Above the signage are boxes of greenery, vines, and flowering plants. Today in early October red geraniums sit in clusters above the outside terrace and bistro tables.

I cross the street and opt for neither the outside nor the red banquettes of the ground floor but rather ask to be seated on the next floor, first floor but our second floor. I read that the French and not the tourists sit here. I'm o.k. being away from those who want to see and be seen. The noise of Boulevard Saint Germain-des-Pres is too much. I pass the empty tables and sit at a corner window table, open to the rooftops of Paris. Outside is a flower box with a pale orchid among the green and rose color flowers. It is like spring and a vertical banner hangs outside with a reverse C and F fluttering in the breeze. The menu is a testament to the literary people who flocked here in the 1940's. They have vanished, but their ghosts remain.

I catch my image in a gold gilded mirror and am quite 'Parisian' today- again in my black leather jacket, always in vogue, and again my mustard - colored long sleeve sweater with a grey/black owl on the front and patches of gray black at the elbows. All I need are my black frame glasses and I can look the part of the intellectual.

I've seen several chic women with animal designed sweaters, understated unique pieces. I might blend in with the sweater but not the shoes. I can't wear their shoes. Again, words of advice don't buy new shoes to wear to Paris. Wear them in first and maybe save the fashionable shoes for special restaurants, exhibits, and jazz clubs.

Wear 'walkable shoes' that you've had for years: AKA sneakers or sandals for your daily walkabouts. Next time I'll spend more on lodgings/apartments in my favorite areas where I can go back to my rooms and rest and change to go back out in the evening. One great night outing is on Thursdays when art galleries have openings. Usually called a vernissage which means varnishing because artists used to finish up their paintings and then put the varnish on. In the process they would invite friends, guests, and viewers to see the paintings before the gallery's opening. Nowadays on Thursdays you can look go on-line and see the vernissage openings. Enjoy cheese and baguettes and wine while mingling and perusing the art.

The very professional waiter hands me a menu and asks if I would like a coffee or a glass of wine. I choose a glass of red wine which he promptly puts on the table as I read the menu decorated with photos and graphics from its long history and an explanation of Café de Flore's origins. I order a salad niçoise which appears quickly on a large plate with crisp lettuce leaves, fresh tomato, potatoes, and anchovies as well as hard-boiled egg wedges. A bed of minced seasoned tuna and homemade mayonnaise rests in the middle. A basket of bread accompanies the lunch and I place a piece of crunchy baguette on the tablecloth. The French just put the bread on the table. That works for me, for there are no extra dishes to wash Also, they do not use butter on their bread so no knives to clean either or extra calories which I can save for dessert or rich sauces. I enjoy looking outside and savoring each mouthful. I feel I have never been so absorbed in just eating and in silence.

People begin to filter in: two young Chinese girls and three older Americans are a few tables over and finally an older French woman with young relatives or acquaintances. All speak quietly and sip their drinks. I wonder if they feel the ambiance and the ghosts and weight of the past. We all linger over meals. I decide to spend more time and order a café and dessert, another Crème Brule which conjures up the magic of this place. Tapping through the golden crust – the crème inside is worth waiting for, like all the good conversations and dreams floating in the atmosphere of this famous café. The Chinese girls catch my eye as I sip my coffee. They motion me up by showing me their camera. Of course, the universal photo. I try speaking in English no luck ...then in a bit of French... no luck - but through pantomiming and nods of the head we communicate. They then indicate if I want mine taken. I nod yes.

They click and for all eternity in my mind's eye, I'll sit in front of a picture of Café de Flore from long ago. Somehow for that one moment I look like I belong in another time. Whenever I look at that picture, I'll remember that day and that moment. I exist in the now and do not think about how I got here or what the future may or may not hold for me .

I walk down the stairs, across the crowded ground floor and out the door into a day that has become a bit less cloudy. The musicians are gone, and I cross and pass their corner on the Boulevard Saint-Germain-des-Pres. So nice just to meander and look at the people and store windows. After a few blocks I cross to the other side and walk up a street that ascends. It's a steep climb after my big lunch – despite the refreshing salad, the bread and crème brulee are holding me down. By the time I get to the top I will have burned it off. Just kidding, I need a marathon for that. When the hill finally ends, it seems to level off at Montagne Saint-Genevieve into Place du Pantheon – an area with wide sidewalks and iron fences. Bearing right, I see a cream amber colored circular building. The area expands to a full view of a huge building with a cupola on top. An iron fence surrounds it to the front entrance of wide stone steps leading to massive doors – the famous Pantheon overlooking Paris confronts me with its tombs of the most famous writers, scientists, and notables. The one I most want to see is Saint Exupery's tomb. He is the author of the only novel we ever read in high school French, the classic, *The Little Prince*.

Inside it is cold and quiet like the crypt that it is. I stand in front of a photo of Antoine Saint Exupery in a WW11 pilot's uniform, an author and a pilot he wrote *Night Flight* which told of the serenity of his flights in 1944 crossing from North Africa to the Mediterranean Sea and the southern coast of France.

It was during one of these missions that he disappeared and was never found until 1998 when a fisherman found a fragment of a pilot's suit and a silver bracelet with Saint Exupery's wife's name on it washed ashore off Marseille. This fisherman, an average Frenchman, knew his country's literature and history. He had found the site where Saint Exupery had crashed more than 75 years ago.

Mesmerized by the sheer force of history, I stand in front of his portrait. I amble out the heavy doors past the standard 21st century security checks and head down the hill toward another set of even taller gates surrounding the Luxembourg Gardens and think of another author this time - the American, Ernest Hemingway, who used to cross through these gardens every day.

On this sunny but cool day I'm appreciative of my leather jacket. So many others are walking, sitting, enjoying the crisp air that too soon will turn cold with winter. I can see why Hemingway liked the Luxembourg Gardens the best in the fall. But it's early yet; flowers still bloom with their pink, orange, and yellow faces. I cross over the pebbled paths, down the steps, past the water fountains and basin in the center. I choose to sit up on a little hill on a red bench looking down on those walking by the basin. I wonder if Hemingway ever sat up here and shuffled his feet through the November leaves. I'd like to be here then since now few leaves have fallen to be crunched by my footsteps.

Day 16

OCTOBER 4

"Half the fun of travel is the esthetic of lostness."

RAY BRADBURY

I relate to this quote because much of the time I am lost – in Paris and on the basic journey of life. I set out on one path and then somehow get to another or realize I should not have set out on that course. Knowing all roads lead somewhere, I begin again but not with my usual petit dejeuner (breakfast) here in my garden studio but out for the renowned Arnaud Delmontel Boulangerie. I would not have known about this bakery were it not for my son who is obsessed with google maps and finding the most interesting places. He emails me that I must not miss the best croissants in Paris – so I head to the Delmontel bakery in Montmartre, the closest to me. Of course, the ultimate question is: "Can you get a bad croissant in Paris?" Nonetheless, my son would be pleased I'm taking his advice.

My apartment is in the 11th and this boulangerie is in the 9th, so it's just a step across to the 18th and Montmartre. It's at 39 Rue des Martyrs. I feel anyone must consider oneself a martyr to travel three metro lines to get a croissant- so it better be 'extraordinaire'. And it is extraordinary. The regular croissants are all gone, but the girl recommends a venoise aux almandes. It's a croissant with a different shape and stuffed with almond paste and slivers of almonds. My son would be proud of me except that I do not take a photo of the croissant. Too hungry, I gobble it all up and even contemplate going back for another. Instead, I ask the young woman to take my photo in front of the bakery.

My son likes food pictures and cooking, but I'm sure he'll settle for me in front of his 'found' bakery. He takes pictures of his restaurant food to remember the moment and archives it so he can find the place in the future. I would rather mark it down in a journal or scratch a reminder in a book. I like pen and pencil records, not digital. So many young people prefer their phones, or iPads which is fine, but I prefer to rummage through a bunch of books and journals than to find what file I put something in on my cell phone or iPad.

As with those I pass on the street who eat their bread or croissants on the way to work, I attempt to blend in, but I don't look like a worker. This is not like in the US at Dunkin Donuts or Starbuck's where one orders a coffee to go then picks up a pastry or donut to go with it and finds a table to eat or takes it in a bag to the office or to munch in the car. Here they just hold the bread or croissant in a thin square of wax paper and bite it as they walk. I do the same as I try to find the Musee des Romantiques, a little museum which houses the works and artifacts of the author Georges Sand. She was an independent woman who took on the name of a man in the 1800's in order to write and live freely.

I get lost on the way but enjoy every morsel of my almond croissant. Just as I am dusting off the last crumbs from my leather jacket, I find a delightful secluded gated lane, Rue du Forchot. I look through the gate and see a storybook lane with little stone unique houses lining the narrow street. I step away so as not to look like a gaping gauche tourist. A well-dressed, silver haired women smiles and passes in front of me and punches in the entrance code. If I had been quick thinking, I would have spoken to her and asked about the lane – perhaps she would have let me in. I usually muster up the words I should have said after the fact. Those are the moments that change destiny or at least alter paths.

I wistfully gaze in and then walk away from the secret path. Further on is a sign that indicates one house in the lane belonged to Jean Renoir, film maker and son of Auguste Renoir- the famous impressionist painter who lived further up the hill on Montmartre. Twists and turns take me to the museum which is a former house of an artist related through marriage to Georges Sand. It was given to the city of Paris to be made into a museum for Georges Sand. It houses paintings, furniture, sculpture, and jewelry from the 1740's-1840's, but it is the house itself that I like.

Hidden on a cobbled stone lane, it has two studios, one on either side. In its time one was for the owner and the other for his brother. The center is comprised of a courtyard that accents the low roof buildings with their old painted doors and windows. A country feel makes this an oasis in the hills of Montmartre, Paris. Today a little 'salon de the' or tearoom lets visitors sit outside beneath the boughs of low branched trees at iron tables and chairs and enjoy the sun as it dabbles through the leaves and kisses the still October roses. All types of people take advantage of this day: mothers and daughters, - grandmothers and children, - couples, - single men and women. Male or female, old or young all enjoy a brief respite in the late afternoon.

From the living to the dead I go, for around the corner is the Cemetery of Montmartre, smaller than Pere Lachaise. It is the last home for many of those who used to live here before the tourists came. I sit near the entrance with an overwhelming feeling of exclusion. I stay long enough to eat an apple, drink from my water bottle, and nod a polite bonjour to the park monitors in yellow jumpsuits. City workers have uniforms – whether street cleaners, garbage men, or parks monitors. They let the uniform state that their job is necessary. R.E.S.P.E.C.T it belts out like Aretha.

$\mathscr{D}ay$ 17

OCTOBER 5

'A woman's always younger than a man at equal years."

ELIZABETH BARRETT BROWNING

There are two open air markets in my arrondissement (neighborhood). The bigger one is near the Bastille on Thursdays and Sundays and on Boulevard Richard-Lenoir on Tuesday and Sundays. I go once a week to stock up on not only vegetables and fruit but also on cooked sausage or couscous dishes that are already made. My place has a microwave so I can just nuke it and not have to get a ton of ingredients to cook on basically a hot plate. The neighborhood women get there as soon as the market opens to get the freshest item, the ones most sought after. I follow them as they wheel their shopping carts – rather like a basket/suitcase on wheels which saves lifting. I just carry a sack rather like a lightweight gym bag, but nonetheless when full, it is very heavy.

I take my time and walk the mini lanes between the stalls. Everything is attractively laid out in orderly rows: fish on ice or oranges in pyramids. The buyer does not touch until ready to buy. Once you select, the grocery man hands you a small plastic bag to put items in. The fish you just point to, but the fruits and vegetables you collect and place in separate sacks. He weighs each and keeps a running tab on a small piece of brown paper which he adds up and announces the total.

In one of the stalls, I hear a boisterous man arguing. The seller at the neighboring stall has a slight grin and shakes his head. A woman customer says something, and the loud guy says in French "It is not your concern, Madame. Shop for your vegetables. Don't worry about me."

She answers, "Monsieur, I do not intend to 'worry' about you, merci beaucoup."

"Madame," what is he so angry about? I ask.

She just gives me the typical French shrug and says, "It's always like this in the market with him. His wife probably threw him out again."

It's rather nice or at least interesting to hear their fervor. I find it unlikely that we hear such impassioned voices at the local Stop and Shop or Big Y. We just pick up our pre-weighed vegetables, chicken, boxes of cereal etc. with no interaction with anyone unless you ask a clerk in the aisle where something is. Nine times out of ten he says, "I don't work here; I'm just stacking the shelves."

One place where the lines are finely drawn are at épiceries (grocery stores) owned by neighborhood shopkeepers. There's a look do not touch even to buy policy. I like to touch everything, so I've learned the hard way.

I exit La Place Bastille and walk up across Avenue Beaumarchais towards home. My sack stocked with tomatoes, onions, garlic, basil, and mushrooms which the merchant picked out for me and eggs for my omelets, two cooked sausages sliced vertically, a cooked chicken, apples, cucumbers, beets, fresh camembert from Normandy plus a few croissants. I stop at a boulangerie near the corner of Rue Saint Sebastien and stick a fresh long baguette into my bag. I feel totally Parisian as it sticks out of my bag, almost like those iconic photos of a boy on a bicycle with a loaf of bread in his back basket or a man walking down a street with two baguettes tucked under his arm.

I return to my studio to put away my provisions which will last three or four days before I go to the market again. I leave out the baguette to make a sandwich of soft camembert and tomatoes. I put on a fresh pot of coffee to go with the most delicious bow shaped pain au chocolat that I bought. It's hard to believe that I might be getting sick of them and I'm only halfway through with my stay.

I push open the French doors to the garden patio and place my purchases on my bistro table. No music serenades me like when I arrived, and the window above is rarely open, but I begin to conjure up a story in my head. Much of my time in Paris is spent observing people as well as places. Often, I think of them as characters in a novel. This morning with my work done I sit with a hot cup of coffee and begin to munch on the chocolate croissant. I would like a partner, or a friend seated opposite me, and we could enjoy the scent of Paris together, talk of the past, plan the day, and conjure up a probable future, but as I am by myself, it's just glorious to sit and dream.

Sandwich made, water in the bag I head out down Passage Saint Sebastien, cross over Avenue Ameliot and walk past the laundromat. I peer in to see if Gary Jules is there. Nope. I walk by and down Avenue Beaumarchais stopping to look in secondhand shops, clothing shops, hardware type stores. I pass cafes and a hotel or two. It's the middle of the week, children are in school, but the street is full of walkers. Everyone here walks, and I join them as I cross over the avenue toward the Marais and one of my favorite spots, le Square Leopold Achille. This time I find it by going down Rue du Pas Mule. The narrow street is lined with a shop of metal artifacts- keys, locks, and curtain rods, pop up clothing stores with coats and jackets, and art and handcrafted jewelry shops.

Further on are little cafes and larger restaurants. I know my way. That's the beauty of renting a place in a neighborhood and then walking outward and touring on a first outing and then back from various points until it becomes your area. I find when I ride or walk with others, I depend on them to navigate. Now if I'm lost, I'm lost. I figure my way back by asking, using paper or online maps. I like to rely on memory and observe the landmarks I pass. I am useless if someone tells me go West then North etc. Instead, tell me to take a left near café Mediterranee and then past Ecole Henri IV etc. I cross through Square Leopold Achille and sit on the bench I now regard as my own. It sits halfway into the square in front of the rose-colored buildings that line the street, but it faces a slate- colored building across the sandy center space in the middle. I'm deciding whether to go to museum Carnavalet and view my paintings of Leonard Foujita or go father to le Petit Palais and sit in those gardens and view my favorites there.

As the sun hides behind a few somber clouds, I decide to take the metro to les Champs Elysees and the Clemenceau stop which puts me a stone's throw from le Petit Palais. I walked out without my umbrella. I made the choice to be packed down like a mule or be free and maybe get caught in the rain. Shopping bags are an entirely different thing - like badges of glory if they have notable logos or designer names. My only notable bag was from Claudalie, the perfume, soap, bath boutique in the Marais district. From their revered vineyards in southern France their products practically promise the fountain of youth . They have recuperative properties made from the residue of their red wine. I'm counting on returning ten years younger.

Out of the subway I run for le Petit Palais before the showers become a deluge. Just as I begin to climb the steps, the skies open and I dash inside just in time. Inside I find my tall vase by Auguste Rodin, a shimmery multicolored green which reminds me of springtime. It is a vase for a proper patio or a marble entranceway in a mansion in the States. If it were for sale, the price tag would be in the thousands, but here it stands in the middle of the entrance area, right in the line of traffic. I'd like to touch it, but I know that's a 'no-no.' Sometimes I can hear my mother's voice in my head, "Diane don't touch." That was her mantra every time we went into a store because I needed to see not only with my eyes but also with my hands. Of course, things broke and that is why I remember the constant admonitions.

I restrain myself and move away from the vase. The room with the Mary Cassatt paintings from 1910 is a better option. They have such soft muted colors perfect for a rainy day. As an American who came to paint in Paris, she painted with the greats. Her subjects were young women with children. She depicted the moments of childhood that pass so quickly and the beauty of young womanhood that vanishes in a heartbeat. They appear to enjoy their lives more back then. Then I remember their lack of choice in so many areas.

I think of Marcel Pagnol's novels of life in southern France at the turn of the 20th century and one of the scenes when the older boy and his brother are following their mother's coffin. "Such is the life of a man. Moments of joy, obliterated by unforgettable sadness. There is no need to tell the children."

He speaks of man not woman – so that in itself puts us in our place. Life is not always better in yesteryear. It is just our assumption that it was. Nonetheless, the message remains in Cassatt's paintings and Pagnol's novels that the present moment is all we have.

How did these artists paint such work? I leave Mary Cassatt and walk to the paint box and easel of Ernest Jules Renoux placed on the floor in front. These objects and a parasol from his studio depict his work habit in the late 1800's to 1932. Did he stand beneath the parasol and pick his spot to paint? The whole concept of painting in "plein-air' (outside) was beginning in his lifetime. Today's artists continue to gather inspiration from the air of Paris. They set up their easels on bridges, in parks, in open squares and anywhere they can catch the light and inspiration from the people of Paris doing their everyday activities.

I have a friend who is an artist. I think about what she would say. But my thoughts and discussions are in my head. She and my children would see the humor in things such as the possibility of me tripping over the painting display in the middle of the floor. It's a true miracle I did not step on it. It's important to laugh. I will sit and people watch and perhaps have a conversation in the open -air cafe in the museum where I can sit in the lush gardens.

Artists or would be artists, for after all this is Paris, are there sitting with their sketch pads. Some sit at the bistro tables outside the café facing the fountain and plants; others sit on the steps between the roman type columns. I sit at a table on the edge of the steps with a view of the dark green waters in the blue tiled pool with frothy ferns. I place my leather journal and coat at the table to save my seat as I stand in line for an expresso. No one will take the leather- bound journal. I am not famous. It's not the suitcase Hemingway left on a train seat by his wife and then walked to another car. When he came back to the car, it was gone. Perhaps the suitcase is on the floor of a Swiss junk shop – but it's been almost 100 years. That's too long to still be around, yet one never knows.

"Madame, what would you like?" The waiter cuts through my reverie. Madame is so much better than 'ma'am'.

"An expresso. It sounds so European, not like saying 'coffee with cream and sugar' at a road stop in the States. It is somehow more exotic – more special.

"Anything else?"

"Something sweet. What would you recommend?"

"This peach flan – the peaches are very fresh."

"Perfect. Thank you."

We continue a mini conversation this dark hair young man and me. He knows I'm American and asks if I live in New York because he has a cousin there. He asks with such a sincerity and sweetness that I don't laugh.

It's crazy how every European thinks you live near or in New York City. I say I do not live in the city, but I was born there. That makes him smile. The idea that I would know his cousin or even the area where he might live makes me smile. Even explaining where Connecticut is and how to pronounce it becomes a culture lesson. I'd have better luck with Massachusetts because they know of the American Revolution, a precursor of theirs.

So, I take my tray of coffee and 'peach custard' and walk down the stone steps, pass the statues, and the columns seemingly from a bygone era. I sit at my table and look at the prism of light from the glass roof which illuminates the entire courtyard and creates a pastoral setting in this sophisticated city. These free settings that Paris has to offer fill me with thankfulness and peace and provide an uncomplicated way to enjoy this city on my own. Each woman can find her own favorite spot: a café, Monoprix's grocery section, a tearoom on Ile Saint Louis, a quiet chapel or church, a cemetery that speaks of yesteryear, a flea market on the edge of the city or the luxurious chairs in Chanel or other designer boutiques where a woman can gaze longingly at exquisite items.

When I return my tray, I ask the waiter for a restaurant recommendation. I tell him I live in the 11th and without missing a beat, he says – Les Fabricants. It serves Southwest French cuisine. I know nothing about that, but he says it's friendly, inexpensive, and fun. He even has a recommendation 'veau montagnarde' - veal stuffed with cheese and mushrooms. I will go home first then go out to the restaurant which is a few blocks from me. It opens at 7 – no happy hours here.

It is so good and too much food. I start with pears in a vinaigrette sauce – the friendly efficient waiter has it in front of me in minutes. The veal takes longer but it's delicious. Of course, the crowd is young. That's no surprise. It's noisy and they interact with one another and not with an older foreigner. However, if I were Meryl Streep or Robert De Niro, I would be part of their conversation. After the delicious meal in a lively spot I return home to write in my place. It's my second novel about a group of women friends from the 1950's /60's who come to Paris to track down a murderer. Since I need to nail down the ambiance and specifics of Paris, I research during the day and write at night. Not all the time, but for me it's a writers retreat without prompts. All good.

Day 18

OCTOBER 6

"Our happiest moments as tourists always seem to come when we stumble upon one thing in pursuit of something else."

LAURENCE BLOCK

Although I escaped the rain drops yesterday and the skies cleared, today is rather grey. It suits my mood. Instead of becoming fearless, I feel isolated and that brings up doubt although I can call family and friends. A free international line is something to look for when you rent since my cell phone I would use only for an emergency. To communicate and discover things I use the internet and e-mail.

Maybe I intrinsically knew I'd need a reprieve from my 'do it alone mindset' because I searched the internet last week and booked my own excursion, a walk through the spots where certain painters painted their famous canvases. Off to a multiple line metro line trip, I must go to Parc Monceau where the tour begins. I grab my food bag, water bottle, and this time my umbrella. I bound down the metro steps of Saint Sebastien. Thirty minutes later I'm at my destination and step out into non-rain skies and a black metal fenced in park of greenery and flower beds in a very residential area. A little boy with no parents in sight whizzes by on his scooter and slides through the partially opened gate. The directions for these on-line minicourses are very exact. I am to meet the group inside an entrance with tall blackish green gated doors decorated in gold. Once inside I find the group.

I hear the refreshing sound of English before I see them. The guide, definitely American and well organized, is a blond woman of a 'certain age'. Under one arm she holds a small portfolio from which she produces computer generated copies of the paintings she will present – on the other arm is her Mary Poppins like sac with an umbrella handle sticking out. She first begins with the history of Parc Monceau. The land was bought by affluent Jewish families who had their great mansions built to border the area. A park for all to enjoy was created in the middle. One specific family had a son who served and died for France in WW1. The father who died afterwards bequeathed great paintings to the Louvre, yet his only remaining child, a daughter, was rounded up by the French police and sent to Auschwitz during WWll. She used to ride with her German officer friends in the park, but that did not save her from Paris' dark years of WWll.

The guide shows us paintings by Monet, Manet, Renoir, Pissarro, and other artists and tells us where in the park or surrounding area they were painted. I find it fascinating how the places have not changed that much in a hundred and fifty years. We get to stand in the exact spots. For Auguste Renoir's umbrellas in blue that was painted in Park Monceau, the dress models of the times had to be accompanied by their mothers or else they were assumed to be prostitutes, and the girls, dressed in gray jackets and skirts, who delivered hats to the fine ladies of the times were called 'gris' girls. They could travel freely with their hat boxes. She showed us Renoir's famous painting of the girls and remarked how their dresses and the painting's background were a blue-gray tone like rain and umbrellas. Eduard Manet's paintings, however, were social commentaries between those looking toward the modern age and those looking back. The one the guide showed was in front of Saint Lazare. The grey of the tracks and iron gating has not changed in 100 years except no steam comes from the trains.

My favorite paintings are those of Gustave Caillebotte who was really an industrial city artist, not a country impressionist like his friends. He also was wealthy in his own right and often bought Manet's and Renoir's paintings to help them support their families. The guide shows us a painting of Caillebotte's brother looking out an apartment window. Then she leads us to the street and points to the apartment window of his brother's building. We also cross the bridge where he painted a well-dressed couple and a man turning around to look at an unaccompanied woman passing by. My favorite painting of people on the street is *Rainy Day* from 1877. A building in the background and much of the painting seems to be in triangular shapes. A formal couple is in the foreground along with the passer-byers. All hold umbrellas. I had an umbrella designed with this painting that my mother had bought from the Art Institute of Chicago where Caillebotte's famous painting hangs.

It was especially wonderful to see and walk the street where this was painted so long ago. It's at an intersection of Gare Saint-Lazare in north Paris. The building in the background reminds me of the Flat Iron Building in New York City. Caillebotte had his apartment in that building. When I returned to the US, I found out his apartment was for sale. Yes, I would have bought it if...

Two and a half hours of walking in the rain let me see the streets as they were once upon a time without the horse drawn carriages but with the same iron- gray gates, skies, and slate rooftops. The eternal gray of Paris lets one appreciate the sunny days, and the history and character in the old gray buildings make them unique and typically Parisian. The group splits into many parts. We leave as we came. I am happy with what I learned about Paris to keep as memories for future rainy days.

I need a coffee so I take a metro line to Notre Dame, and I cross in front of the Statue of Charlemagne and over to Shakespeare and Company on the corner just off the bridge. The coffees are terribly expensive but worth it. I'm standing in line and an English woman says to her husband, "I'm not buying a pot of tea for $6.00". They leave and I move ahead in the line. The waiters and clerks all speak English so if she offended this waiter, she knew it, but he is probably a student at the Sorbonne and gets to practice his English and does not have to be concerned with profit margins. I however indulge in a luxury – a 'white coffee' which is sort of like a café crème but much larger with lots of coffee and an abundance of milk like only the French do. I sit outside under a table with an umbrella with a view of Notre Dame and sip my hot coffee which they brought out to me at a cost of $5.00. Great coffee and a delightful chat with a young Frenchman and his girlfriend. Of course, much of it was about New York City where he had an internship and learned English. He spoke of his love of New York and I of Paris. What could be better?

$\mathcal{D}$ay 19

OCTOBER 7

Art enables us to find ourselves and lose ourselves at the same time."

THOMAS MERTON

I decide my next few days will be my 'art circuit' days: the Louvre, Musee de Tokyo, and the Momartan Museum. First the classics – the Mona Lisa. No metros for this morning. The day is crystal perfect – sunny and clear. Water and sandwich on board I walk down to the Rue de Rivoli- I stop in shops along the way. I had googled vintage stores and found a few "Frippery" shops as they are called. I enter a crowded one and barely get through the door. There's a bin or rather a cardboard box of 5 euro items and then another of 10 euro. The rest of the merchandise is jammed into racks. I spot leopard in the 5-euro box. I have a running joke with a friend – never enough leopard – after all it's a wardrobe basic. This shred of a blouse was anything but – a made in China label with no style and missing most of its buttons. I entertain the idea of going to one of the vast flea markets on the edge of Paris to find the real stuff although this store probably has real fleas. As I exit, I check my ankles.

By the time I get to the Louvre my water is gone. I enter through the Pyramid's glass ceilings. It's so magnificent to look up at this modern glass

Pyramid designed by Chinese American architect I.M.Pei in 1989. It was so controversial then- why put a modern piece in the ancient courtyard of the kings of France? But when I enter and look up and see the surrounding wings and rooftops of the Louvre, the contrast is extraordinary. I stand below with a reverse pyramid above my head and persuade a group of Spanish young men to take my photo. We communicate in Spanish, French, and English. The world community is so small, and peoples' emotions are the same. They are as delighted to be in Paris as I am. I have my single photo of that day and they have their group photo. We say adios and go on our ways.

The many wings of this museum house so many works that you have to decide what you want to see. A guide told me she spent 30 days in the Louvre just walking through room after room and corridors after corridors trying to learn about the works; she still did not see all of it. I have one day, and I do not intend to rush.

"Where is the Mona Lisa?" I ask a guard.

"La Jaconde, the Mona Lisa, is in wing Denon, on the first floor," he smiles.

Of course, he has it down pat as does the sign and arrow pointing the way right in front of me. Every tourist in the world enters and asks that question, but to his credit there is no superiority in his manner just a very professional attitude.

"Merci" I say and head off to see her once again. I saw the Mona Lisa in 1965 when one could get close and personal. Now it is different. In my mind's eye it had no glass around it and was not hung so high. Few people were there. However, I googled it to discover that she had been behind glass since 1960. I must have distorted my memory, but as I approach today an entire crowd is in front of me. Luckily, I can see over their heads - high up where she views us. Still, my impression is the same. She appears so small. It is certainly 'not much to do about nothing", but she has such a strong persona that nothing can compete with how my mind elevated her to be much larger and grander than she actually is.

I stand in her presence and need to move since I cannot stand waiting with the crazies who just use their cell phones to view the world. Enjoy the painting and buy a postcard. I move on to other rooms and other paintings. I decide to just turn right or left on a whim. Too much to see and absorb. I soon find my way to the Sully Wing and down the stairs to the foundation of the Louvre. Here in the Medieval Louvre, it's like exploring the ruins of its original castle. The Louvre was the home of the kings of France. As each one reigned, he added rooms or wings to expand the showcase of the monarchy. The original King, Philippe August built his fortress and the walls around Paris. Beneath the ground one can see the ruins of the castle that existed from the late 1100's until the early 1500's.

I follow the footpath and roped-in areas beneath this area of the Louvre – the dark amber light reflects off the stone and creates the ambiance of another time. Part of the original tower is here – massive in its circumference. There is a model of the castle as it once was – towers and moat included. Archways lead from one chamber to the next until one enters the Egyptian collection. Statues, pyramids, and the living conditions illustrate the continuance of the history of man and woman. I hear nothing but silence and the occasional footsteps of someone else walking through time.

It becomes claustrophobic. I need air and sky. Stairs are not fast enough. I take an elevator to a higher floor and look out the King's windows to the courtyard below. I can see the pyramid entrance and the lines of windows from another wing across the way. But still, it's not enough; I head outside to find gardens of color. The Tuileries were the gardens of the kings. I walk under the petit Carousel into these greens of the Louvre which extend all the way to La Place de la Concorde. Everything is green – grass and trees border the wide path that cuts through the garden. On either side flowers bloom and statues watch as children run to the fountain to sail their boats.

Dozens of people sit in the metal chairs around the fountain. I hear Spanish, English, Italian, German, and of course French. Everyone is living in the moment of this superb day. Most are eating by the fountain, but I want to eat my sandwich in a more tranquil place. I get up and follow a wide path which has smaller paths with tree scattered lanes off either side. I bear to the left near a wooden bridge – much like a Claude Monet Garden painting. Tall grasses border the pond, and a few people rest in the sun. I find a secluded chair in front of statue of a heron. I pull out my sandwich and water and begin to eat. The statue turns his head. This real bird is standing on thin pipe legs in the middle of the water. A man sits in the only remaining chair. And begins to open his lunch sack. He says "bonjour... il fait beau," Ouais," I respond with the colloquial 'ouais' rather like our 'yeah' not 'oui'.

I glance over and note his impeccable grey suit with tapered narrow legs and pointed black leather shoes. He makes no more comment but eats his lunch in a precise manner. I think he must be on an office break. I wonder what he does with the rest of his lunch hour – or is it an hour... or two. Probably an expresso at some café. I sit for more than an hour ... in the sun, watching the motionless bird and children across the way playing by the far shore across the bridge. For me, the temperature calls for an ice cream not a coffee and I wander over to the right of the wide path to a colorful playhouse type structure. Children stand in line to be served ice cream cones; I join them. Perfect! I buy a boule, one scoop, of salted caramel ice cream , which is extremely expensive, small, but so good. The taste and scenery I will remember for a lifetime. Crazy that expression. I have already spent a lifetime; therefore, I should just say a memory for the rest of my life. So be it.

Day 20

October 8 Tokyo museum and Gallica

There is one voyage, the first, the last, the only one."

THOMAS WOLFE

Another day begins with a long trek to get to my destination, the Museum of Modern Art in the Palais de Tokyo. I just reread this; it sounds so blasé.

Just another day - wake up woman, this is Paris not another day at the office. This office is the most beautiful city in the world and my time is my own. I pack up another bag lunch on my journey through Paris to eat somewhere in this glorious city. I do this so that I can enjoy as much as possible - to take it all in at my leisure. From the last metro stop I arrive onto the Avenue de New York – ah, the city where I was born and where my mother worked as a secretary

when she was a young woman. She delighted in walking the avenues to window shop and sometimes actually bought a dress during her lunch hour.

Here I am on her name sake avenue walking toward the Eiffel Tower and the museum of modern art.

I did not know the Eiffel Tower was here because I had seen it from another angle. I think of Meg Ryan in the movie French Kiss always trying to see the Eiffel Tower and just missing it. I walk down the avenue in September and pass a few planters of yellow roses and sunflowers before I see her, so quiet and formidable, The Eiffel Tower, not Meg Ryan.

I climb up steep back steps to the Tokyo Museum and pass some apartment exteriors painted a mélange of green, rose, and yellow. Gardens with vegetables in the middle of the city right off the Seine showcase tomatoes, squash and cucumbers. A little sign bordered in ink proclaims it as "La Parcelle Rose" – a rose colored plot.

Delightful to step out of this industrial building and pick your own dinner.

Halfway up the steps I turn to get a full view of the Eiffel Tower before continuing to the top. I look right and see the entrance into the museum. Another free one – amazing how France has no entrance fees for many museums or that there is a free day or a 'retraite' admission – an admission for retirees. You could be 30 or 60 but if you are retired from the work force ... the crazy nonstop sidewalks of work 'work', you qualify for reduced admission. That describes me. My sidewalks are just for meandering.

I enter a room that takes my breath away. The walls display huge paintings – colors so expansive you can almost see the mind of God. Some are comprised of geometric shapes – circles, squares, rectangles; it does not matter, for all are mixed to make the viewer see beyond the canvas into another world. Muted ones with swirls of mint green, pale blue, and lavender show motion in infinity. I keep walking around the room to absorb it all but know I never can. Finally, I exit through the cafeteria onto a sunny terrace. The sky is a cloudless blue and the Eiffel Tower shoots into the atmosphere. Few people see the tower from this vantage point.

I place my bottled water on a table in the sun and go back inside to order an expresso to sip and a dish of yogurt with berries to eat al fresco as I enjoy the view. On the stone wall separating the terrace from the courtyard and the Seine below is a large pigeon. All I can do is marvel at this scene. The barges follow the current, passing in front. The fat pigeon sits like a true Frenchman, assured of his superiority as he alternates his view from the people eating to the Seine meandering by as it has for centuries. The Seine and the Tower stand to monitor all below, and I glance across the stone terrace beyond the pigeon to the sidewalk below to view Paris at its best – serene, majestic, and impassable. The façade is one of true beauty. I see how she must have stood during those dark years of war from 1940-44.

This museum of course did not exist then but these apartments that border this place must have. And what those people saw one can only imagine. But I am here now… not then and lucky to be here and brave to go on my own as a friend told me. The question is why not? If all we have is this journey in life, we must take advantage of whatever opportunities present themselves to us.

"You must see the furniture rooms here…to die for." A black raven hair creature murmurs to the man sitting across from her. Either her 'papa' or her sugar daddy' even the term 'sugar daddy' fits the rooms I enter. Such glorious retro art deco from the 1930's – sleek python chairs, a leopard chaise lounge, and a lithograph of a leopard on the wall seems like a stage set for the shiny metal desk with tomato red shelves in the middle of the room. Even today it would look perfect in a super expensive office. I imagine who might have used these objects. I think that a woman designer, a lady in red, willing to take risks for women in the next century designed this.

I step out into the sunshine behind the high heeled black raven – whose black silk dress hugs her hips as she minces down the steps holding onto the 'sugar daddy's' arm - yes, most assuredly not her 'papa'.

Off to the Palais Galliera the building across the way that looks like it stepped out of roman times with its six stone columns in front of its stone edifice. From a distance it welcomes as a gladiator might have warranted from bygone years. Delicate measured gardens are parceled out amid the expansive lawns. Today it proclaims the couturier Azzedine Alaia, the famous designer of the 1980's whose artful tailoring, style, and eternal black silhouettes are followed by today's fashionistas.

The man in charge of the tickets is far from a fashionista. He peers at me from his glasses halfway down his nose.

"Billet retraite."

"Yes, unfortunately a ticket for a retiree."

"Non, Madame. You deserve it. You have earned it."

"Really?"

"Oui Madame"

Yes, for sure.

"Madame you have earned it."

I smile and nod my head yes. All the moments I have worked have led me here. I should get a discount. I wonder if sleek raven lady has already been here without a discount although sugar daddy would qualify.

Has she already passed by the corseted black and form fitting bodices of dresses and gowns? I must admit she would wear them fabulously and have places to go in them. I would not be wearing such in suburbia. I try to take a photo of one of the slinky dresses but one of the guards says, 'Non, Madame," and shakes his finger as though I do not understand Non. Only in Paris. I love it.

I love all the creations even though I would barely get one side of my torso in one. "Ah. C'est la vie." No croissants tomorrow.

$\mathcal{D}ay$ 21

OCTOBER 9

"To travel is to take a journey into oneself."

DANNY KAYE

My mother liked to travel, and she would have loved that I am here on my own. I think about her because her birthday is soon. She was born in the same year and practically the same day as Edith Piaf, but Piaf has been gone more than 50 years and my mother but 10. Nonetheless as I travel into myself, I think of them both. What were their regrets? Piaf claimed she had none ... 'je ne regrette rien.' I know my mother must have had a few, but if so, she never mentioned any. I think women and men of her generation just 'stuffed everything down'. They had the Depression and a the War to get through. There was no Facebook, Instagram, or twitter to put everything out there. Their motto was that of Winston Churchill's "When you're walking through Hell, keep on moving."

I am the generation after Churchill but during John F. Kennedy. I wish I could have been like Piaf, but I have had a few or rather quite a few regrets. I was not a hippie, but I should have dropped out of college – not to go on some commune, but to backpack to France with a boy from school. I was a coward. I felt I could not take the risk. I had no safety net, no plan B, if something went awry. Credit cards did not exist. I would have to ask for money if I got in a jam, yet my mother had none to wire. I never left on that trip, the might-have-been Jack Kerouac journey into self through Paris and beyond. In fact, that would have been the same year Kerouac was in Paris making his journey – 1966.

I am here now, however, 'sans un mec' (without a guy) for support, love, and laughter. I can't go back. I have only the present – I do not regret that I chose to be here, so I take a deep breath and dive into today's life.

I find myself measuring my years against others since I am in the outfield of life and shorter on time than I used to be. I have acquired a bad habit. I figure out the lifespan of the painters in the museums, resistance fighters on the placards on buildings, and writers who lived in Paris. How old were they when they died; am I younger or older than they? My father died on October 13. He was younger than I am now. Too many deaths which of course are a part of life, but as I age it hits me- how every year is taken for granted like it's a given. When do you stop buying Christmas paper and cards on sale after Christmas for the next season? Is that optimism, wastefulness, or silliness? Pay full price next year. Spend the money today - Live now. You might not be here next year.

These moments are all we have. I travel for me but also for those who won't or can't - for those who are a part of me. I see things through their eyes and for their eyes. My precious Julian, my son's son, died before he was born, and his wife, my strong sad daughter-in-law who gave birth to their first baby who never got a chance to breathe - to live. I saw his name on the ancient church, St Julien le Pauvre near Shakespeare and Company on the left bank.

I see his name, my sweet Julian, throughout Paris. I see too many babies on the street who should be him.

I see places where I would have taken him had he grown up. Such is a place in a distant 16ᵗʰ arrondissement, the Monmarttan Museum. It is full of paintings by the impressionists. They have always been my favorite; I've showed many to my grandson Sebastian at various museums in the United States and was planning to show Julian the same and to take them both to Paris. So today I view them for both. As I walk past the great expanse of so many flowers – irises, roses, waterlilies, I send my thoughts to both boys – one is right by my side now in spirit, the other back home in the USA. I miss them both so much. But I'm seeing everything for me as well as for them. I can tell Sebastian about it when I return home.

To see these paintings in books is amazing but then to be slapped in the face with the actual ones makes it hard to believe they are real. I just sit on a bench and let my eyes soak in the colors and the light of each rose, iris, or waterlily. The muted pinks, whites, and greens portray eternal summer, days of forever sunshine.

A guard tells me these used to be at Giverny, Monet's home outside of Paris, but after Monet's last son's death in 1966 they were given to the Monmarttan. Had that son journeyed back into time and looked at a waterlily painting by his father perhaps he could see his father painting it in the summer sun as his stepsister held a parasol over their father's head.

I have traveled far to have this experience and revelation that our summer days are but numbered. I stand up and move upstairs to see Monet's "L'Impression du soleil levant". This was the painting he had submitted to the exhibition of his fellow painters in 1874. This famous sunrise over the Seine was ridiculed and not deemed to be 'real art'. The critics called in an impression. He and his fellow painters were lumped together under that new name, Impressionists.

This painting's size, 2ft by 2 ft., startles me. It was so important in what it represented and depicted that I thought it would be large. Manet's even smaller portrait of Berthe Morisot affects me the same. It's funny how the mind and heart conjure up its own vision of 'reality'.

Time to travel out. I can leave. The guards cannot. How do they feel being inside everyday staring at works that belong to the world? Do they have favorites – or is it simply a job like any other job, and they don't think of the history and beauty that surrounds them. Then like me they go home – out the front door of this beautiful stone mansion by the quiet streets and the park and other mansions that surround the Monmarttan. Now everyone walks through the Neuilly-Passy quarter of the 16[th,] one of the most exclusive and expensive pieces of real estate. This plot of land in Paris is known for its famous ladies in pearls and simple black dresses. I pass a few elderly women, like Coco herself as she heralded in the 1920's. They are wearing chic Channel suits with pearl trimmed jackets. The grand dames own pearls encircle their necks. They and I seem to be the only ones walking in this exclusive district. An occasional man in a pressed grey suit with a white starched shirt hobbles by with a cane. As I walk, I pass by a phone booth – probably one of the ten still left in Paris. Do these men and women of another era know about cell phones? Do these booths still take francs and not euros? I should have walked inside and looked.

$\mathscr{D}ay$ 22

OCTOBER10

"Every exit is an entrance somewhere."

TOM STOPPARD

I will soon be exiting this city that I love so much. You always remember the first time you do something or saw something, but when you're living life you do not say, "I want to remember these days because who knows if this will be the last time I'll see Paris."

The cliché of the 'ugly American' is a thing locked in the past – after WW11 and the stereotype of the camera-around-the-neck accessory of the 1950's American tourist. Today other nationalities with high tech digital cameras, smart phones or the latest iPhone have upstaged us. However, we have a bad rap on the political stage. You almost want to say you are Canadian to avoid any eavesdropping terrorist. Just kidding. That mind set must be dismissed. We travel because we must view the beauty of other places and people and connect to all humanity. We can't be afraid that a train, plane, or automobile will blow up or a van will come careening down the street. It can happen on Main Street U.S.A. You must be observant and defiant.

This is almost my last day in the market. I feel more comfortable shopping like this than in the air conditioned, music filled football field supermarkets with their hermetically sealed packages back home. I like looking at the produce and fish and figuring out what I want and the price in dollars vs euros. The markets also sell clothing and household items. I had a mini conversation with a man who sold sweaters and rain jackets. He asked how far away I was from New York because he too had a cousin there. He said how he wanted to see New York City. His fascination with New York is like mine for Paris.

"We gave you the Statue of Liberty. I want to see it. Have you?"

"Yes, when I was a child. Have you gone up the Eiffel Tower?"

"Non" He shrugged his shoulders.

After all Paris is only Paris to him, and New York is magic. I wave good- bye and return to the streets I know so well by now. I plop my cucumbers, peaches, and cheese on the counter and try to skype home... Voila no internet.

'Great' and the phone line to call the landlady also does not work. It's probably bundled together like in the USA. I walk into a café where a young man is setting up for lunch. He dials the number and lets me talk with Francine who blithely tells me they must not have received the payment yet for service. That 'Oh well attitude amazes me... except of course if the shoe's on the other foot. Then it's a high volume 'discussion' on the merits of this vs that.

I decide to get my head in another direction; I head for the literary 6th arrondissement again. Hemingway, Gertrude Stein, Fitzgerald, and Sartre/ De Beauvoir will empty my head from being put adrift with no internet to communicate. After all I am not on a desert island, just the island of Paris. I will survive. I exit the metro at Vavin in the 6th and walk into the 7th to get chocolate at Hugo and Victor. It's a great name for this exclusive shop that sells chocolate in little black boxes that look like books, emblazed with gold letters *Victor & Hugo* on top.

Walking through the Luxembourg gardens, I see the bushes and trees starting to change color. I think of what Hemingway thought while shuffling through the leaves on his way to Montparnasse. Often, he stopped at La Closerie des Lilas, but there is no more lilac tree just a sign inside to commemorate where the America sat in the 1920's. I don't open the book box of chocolate but rather the white folded paper pouch that contains three chocolates. I select one and let in melt in my mouth and promise myself I will not eat the whole bag and then begin on the black box.

In this area, the 6th, I easily find the former house and studio of Ossip Zadkine set secluded in a garden filled with his sculptures. He was a famous sculptor in the mid 1900's and his former garden has stone and metal figures with cubistic and lean lines. They are bold and alive. I can almost hear them talking to one another as I wander back and forth in the warm October air. Two stark figures with arms around one another's shoulders and mammoth hands clasping one another is a rendition of the Van Gogh brothers. It is forceful and moving. His sculptures are placed against the white walls of the house and outside under trees as strong as his work.

I step inside to the all-white rooms with birch wood floors; It's a jewel highlighted with a variety of wooden, stone and metal works clearly labeled and most with photographs of Russia in the early 1900's. They are stark and representative of the turmoil of those years. His work from 18-inch pieces to 7-foot ones are primitive yet futuristic. They remind me of Picasso's works and speak to me of the joy and despair of humanity. His works have crossed the decades and speak profoundly of mankind. I stay until it closes and then wander down the streets – turning this and that way on a whim, I see majestic, delightful apartment buildings on tree lined streets and wonder who is fortunate enough to live there.

I also love passing schools – ecoles maternelles (elementary schools), lycées (usually middle schools) and colleges (high schools). I hear children playing in the high walled courtyard playgrounds. The older students lock their skateboards and bikes to barriers along the sidewalks bordering the schools. One school for older students was called les Alsaciens – named for the families who had come to Paris from Strasbourg near the German border. I like seeing the older students leaning up against the building or eating their lunch in a nearby park. They lie in the sun until the classes begin again. Some read. Some study. Some chat. It all seems very civilized and not directed by bells and school guards. Students are given freedom to act accordingly. Helicopter parents do not seem to exist.

$\mathcal{D}ay$ 23

OCTOBER 11

"You do not travel if you are afraid of the unknown; you travel for the unknown that reveals you with yourself."

ELLA MILLART

Today would have been my mother's birthday and I remember how she loved to travel, meet new people, and learn new things. She did not go on her own but with groups and prearranged courses and tours. In those days it was very reasonable. She retired and traveled by taking courses at universities. Everything was so cheap. The same tours cost $5,000 for 7 days not including transportation. Hers were longer and cost but hundreds. Even at that price she had to budget and save, but she made travel and learning a priority.

Edith Piaf, France's Judy Garland, died 50 years ago on this day – October 11. My mother has been gone 8 years – my father forty-seven but I still catch myself thinking that I must call one of them to ask a question or tell them about someone. It has been 50 years since JFK was killed. It passed in the blink of an eye. I cannot seem to slow time down. I wish my mother had prepared me for this aspect of adult life when you remember more about the past than what you did yesterday.

When I was young, no one died. I never thought about death - only about life and what tomorrow would bring. Now too many deaths have touched my life and I realize how I took the years as a given. I realize now that the young do not contemplate death. They just expect every day to be here, and everything is exciting because it is new. The question is if we knew how many days we have, would that make a difference in how we spend them? And if you have but few, would you want to know?

Life is not necessarily fair and sometimes it is tragic. What happens is often not expected. It is what one does afterwards that defines one's life. Tragedy forces one to pick up the pieces and put one foot in front of the other. Today I will go to the Musee D'Orsay where my mother and daughter-in-law would find beauty. It is an old railroad station built between 1808-1900 on the left bank of the Seine that was turned into a museum in 1987 to house the works of Monet, Manet, Van Gogh, and other impressionists. The sun shines through the old glass railroad station windows and lights the inside to accentuate the light in the paintings.

$\mathcal{D}ay$ 24

OCTOBER 12

'No man is an island.'

THOMAS MOORE

I am walking back to the Hotel de Ville and going to enter through the main doors. I don't care if I run into the disagreeable guard because he will not remember one particular tourist, nor do I intend to ask him any questions. I know the Hotel de Ville is not a hotel but rather the town hall of Paris. Unlike our humble town halls that are sometimes grouped with senior centers or libraries this one stand tall and imposing with massive pillars and gold trimmed gates surrounding the stone walls.

The entrance is up many imposing stone steps made of massive rocks. Few public buildings are handicapped accessible. This one is no exception. At the top of the stairs, I enter through the imposing doors to a series of rooms with large canvases and series of smaller ones on adjacent walls. What strikes me is the primitiveness and bright colors of each one. They are painted by the emotionally or mentally impaired from the schools and hospitals throughout Paris. They are magnificent – full of passion, beauty, and pain. One student's comment is on the wall near his/her artwork, "I love putting the things I draw in color, otherwise it would be sad"

The walls of the rooms are bright blue or black, so the vivid paintings stand out. A profusion of yellows, oranges, and red tell the stories of ballet dancers like Degas' or modern dancers, white and in a circle like Matisse's. Others look like they came from Africa: suns, animals, and bolts of sword like shapes cutting through the design.

The place is crowded. Viewers, trying to capture the meaning or emotion of a work, stand in front of a painting for a long time. Although the colors are like Van Gogh's and the shapes rather like modern art, they are not done by the famous but rather the forgotten or unfortunate children of Paris. Art lovers have come to appreciate them and bask in the beauty of art and humanity.

I too go back to my favorites and stand to capture the feelings of these young artists who somehow use the medium to express their joy or anguish. Perhaps they cannot talk or cannot talk with sense, so they are shown how to paint in order to communicate. They touched my heart and I leave to walk over to the Ile de la Cite where Notre Dame dominates and to give thanks.

These are the streets of tourist shops. Everyone who visits Paris visits Notre Dame and walks around the area to buy mementoes. I too am here to buy souvenirs for my son. He uses them as prizes for the kids in his French classes. He gave me a budget so I have to buy as many Eiffel Towers as I can. Although the stores basically have the same merchandise, the prices vary. I look through the bins on the sidewalks in front of the stores. I buy a handful of little metal Notre Dame key chains. The little cathedrals have an eyepiece to peek inside and see the interior lite up from the light. I buy from the shop that has ten for $15 rather than $2 apiece. I grab two more handfuls of Mona Lisa, Sacre Coeur, and Arc of Triumph. So many things catch my eye as I hang on to my pocketbook and my sac of keychains.

I walk on the outer sidewalk now because the streets are too crowded. I'm heading for the back of the cathedral where the expansive buttresses provide support for the church. Gargoyles project from the roof. It's the French version of rain gutters. I realize I can go inside the gated walls of Notre Dame, and I enter a little park which is dwarfed by the impressive church. I do not need to go inside. The peace and serenity I can feel from here. I sit on a stone bench and look up at the spires, buttresses, and rooftops of Paris' oldest building. Paris began here on this tip of the island.

I cross over Pont Neuf to the right bank and walk in the direction of the Louvre. The day is sunny with white clouds dotting the sky. I walk towards the Tuileries, located between the Louvre on the rue de Rivoli, crowded with traffic and people, and the Place de la Concord in the lst arrondissement. It is not good to breath in the odious fumes and the Seine is a stone's throw. I walk until I see the greenery of the garden and enter.

Now it is a large public garden, one of the biggest and oldest in the capital, with a history that dates back to the 17th century. Parisians take advantage of such beauty and space. Today is no exception, it is full of life and the shouts of children.

Centuries ago, this was the land for tile factories, but Catherine de Médicis, the widow of King Henri II, had the palace of the Tuileries constructed. It became the residence of many rulers such as Henri IV, Louis XIV, and Napoléon Bonaparte. An Italian Garden was built on the west side of the palace. In 1664 Louis XIV had the famous landscaper of the time André Le Nôtre redesign the gardens in a very popular French style of the time. As I walk through the pathways, I can imagine where the palace once stood. Two kings and a hundred and twenty years later, Louis XVI and Marie-Antoinette fled through the Tuileries Garden during the uprising of 1789, and attempted to take refuge in the palace, but the revolutionaries captured them and took them back to the Palace of Versailles.

Now the only ones running are children laughing and playing between the statues in these gardens. The sky is blue and smeared with white clouds and a feeling of joy floats through the gardens. The terror of the Revolution, almost four centuries ago, is impossible to imagine in today's Paris. The only shouts and screams are those of vendors from North Africa. They sell paper birds that fly through the air and many tiny Eiffel towers in silver, gold, copper, and orange colors which hang in cords from their belts.

I approach them one at a time to find out the price.

"Madame, do not bother. Ne vous en inquiétez pas. Don't worry I give you the best price." A tall thin very dark young man says.

We negotiate, and I buy twenty-five of various colors for my son. He will be thrilled, but I wonder how I am going to pack and transport all of this to the US. My sac is so heavy that I can barely carry it. I did have the foresight to bring a small backpack, so I put them all in there and hoist it on my back. Much easier.

I see a carousel ahead and walk toward it. I am looking for a spot to sit and eat. Almost to the Place de la Concord, the Eiffel Tower looms in the distance. Stone benches encircle a sandy area where the paths seem to end. I sit on the outer edge beneath some greenery near a statue of Rodin's Kiss. Beyond this is the frenzied traffic of the Place to la Concord where 230 years ago Louis XVl was beheaded by the guillotine. Now the President of France lives in the Elysée Palace right off this circle which extends beyond to the Arc of Triumph and the Champs des Elysees.

Being a modern woman, I do not have to lift up my heavy long ankle length skirt and petticoats and traipse on laced up leather boots to the small stall across the sandy circle. I smell crepes and coffee. I stand at the end of the line and look at the chalkboard for choices.

"Madame what would you like?"

"What would you suggest?"

« Crepes, » he points to the chalk board above his head."

"O.K. One cheese and one Nutella and un café noir s'il vous plait."

« Bien sur »

He is certainly right. I have my crepes and coffee in my hand and nothing to carry. My sack is on my back; I sit near "The Kiss" and gaze out at the Eiffel Tower across the Seine.

The best food is when you are hungry, and you pick what you want at that moment. It suits your mood and appetite precisely. I eat the one with protein first and then the chocolate Nutella one for dessert. Not the South Beach diet but who wants that in Paris as one sits in the sun and open air. Cheese and chocolate is the best. No wine but coffee suits the bill.

I rest and observe for a long time. I look over the walled edge and notice an old woman in wedge heels riding a bike through the traffic. Her bike baskets are filled with flowers and two long baguettes. Her skirt is pulled up and her hair is pulled back. She is a woman with a purpose. I have a feeling she knows who she is. She seems fearless. I bet no one tells her what to do. I like that.

The young meander and then there are the teenagers. Several in their black motorcycle boots minus the motorcycle step with determination kicking stones along the way through the sandy terrain. Black leather jackets and skinny black jeans complete their look as cigarettes dangle from their lips. The leader of the pack with his slicked black hair flips his cigarette butt to the ground and the kid behind crushes it with his boot. It could be a scene from a movie – so cliché so perfect.

A Thomas Wolfe type follows a distance away. He wears a black fedora tilted to one side, A black velvet loose blazer and black wool pants complete his look. The only contrast is his white hair that falls out from beneath his hat. I wonder if he knows who Thomas Wolfe was, but then again, he is French and looks like a literary type. Perhaps though he is a poseur – an

American who likes to live in another time and place. If I did not have this heavy schoolgirl backpack, I'd saunter over and ask.

Instead, I check out the Orangerie Museum with its windowless imposing wall of stone right behind me. I turn the corner, see the huge columns, and entrance door. Napoleon 111 had the Orangerie built in 1852 to store the citrus trees of the Tuilleries garden from the cold in the winter. Constructed mainly out of glass, it allowed the light in for the orange trees. In 1871, the Orangerie became the property of the State, which used it for orange trees as well as for music concerts, art expositions, contests and even dog shows until 1922 when the use was to be a showcase for Monet's paintings. Today the Orangerie is an art gallery of impressionist and post-impressionist artists. Inside I find two large oval rooms with glass panels on the roof to allow the light to shine on Claude Monet's eight long panels of water lilies. He had painted these in the last years of his life as a gift for the State, and he helped design the two oval rooms in which they are displayed. He demanded skylights to catch the rays of the sun as they travel across the building from east to west.

Everything is white except his waterlilies. I feel as though I am sitting by his pond in Giverny as the seasons change. The bench is metal and mimics the oval shape of the rooms. I just sit and look - mesmerized by the colors, light and moment captured in the painting. One room is spring/ summer, and the other is fall/winter. I walk parallel to each and feel the change of seasons. I wish I were the only viewer then I could pretend they were mine. However, dozens are here. Everyone is silent. We are in awe. I know I cannot stay forever. I journey downstairs to the other rooms where two of my favorite Renoirs, the ones of two young girls, hang side by side. One is of just their faces and shoulders and the other is of them sitting side by side at the piano. Both portraits have them dressed in fine hats and dresses They remind me of my two daughters: one blond and one brunette. Copies of these have been on my walls for years.

I wander through the rooms to look at other Renoirs, and paintings by Gauguin, Cezanne, Picasso, and many other famous artists. The Orangerie is a jewel, so small and intimate that you feel you are in a private home waiting for the hostess to arrive with glasses of champagne.

$\mathcal{D}ay$ 25

OCTOBER 13

"If you are lucky enough to have lived in Paris as a young man - (or maybe Woman my dear Mr. Hemingway), then wherever you go for the rest of your life it stays with you for Paris is a moveable feast."

ERNEST HEMINGWAY

I only realized a few years ago that my father and Hemingway were born in the same year, 1898 . That is so crazy – not last century but the century before. I never thought to ask him about his favorite books. I was just beginning my own life as an adult when he died on October 13, 1965. There were so many questions I never asked him and so many things about his past he never shared. My mother, much younger than he, was the reader. My father and I shared no literary interest between us. He liked cowboy movies so that is what we shared, an interest in the Wild West. My perceptions came from T.V. shows and movies that we would see. Our move to California brought dreams of cowboys and Indians, open land with buffalos and a primitive 'barebones' life. The reality of California in the 1950's did not meet my expectations. I would see a glimpse of the 'other' west of yesteryear in an old mission or ranch, but our groceries still came from supermarkets or roadside stands. It must not have met his expectations either because we only stayed two years before moving back east.

Perhaps I'll feel his presence at the movies, so I decide to go to the Musee Cinémathèque in Bercy in the 12th arrondissement. It takes a few metro stops and a lot of walking to get to this outer edge of Paris. The stone and glass building looks like a college classroom building. It holds all the apparatus of the first film productions. Old cameras, lights, film projectors and props tell the story of how movies began. He would like this because of all the gadgets and short film clips in grainy black and white. Jean Cocteau is featured. My father would have had no idea who he was; he did not take film study classes that were so popular at college and high school campuses in the 1970's/80's. He did, however, know the story of *Beauty and the Beast.* This was one of Cocteau's masterpieces, *La Belle et La Bete* which had a very scary beast and the first special effects of the times.

After a few hours of listening, viewing, and reading explanations of the how to's of cinematography I move on to an open area – no concrete and glass but trees, pathways, terraces, rope bridges and stone 'castles'. Parc des Buttes Chaumont is not a manicured park of flowers and pristine lawns but rather an Indiana Jones terrain of ruggedness. My son told me to visit this less touristy part of Paris. Walking to it from the closest metro stop, I feel the slight upward grade of the sidewalks. This is a working- class neighborhood – rather like going through Hell's Kitchen in New York City before it became gentrified. Men, heads bent down over their expressos with cigarettes hanging from their lips sit at the tables outside rundown cafes. Women with scarves over their heads hang on to their children's hands as they pull laundry baskets up the steep sidewalks skirting garbage cans along the way.

I look up the street to see the park loaming ahead. The neighborhood becomes nicer with cleaner buildings with their carved colorful doors and gridiron balconies. Flowers still bloom in the entrance way pots and window boxes. I walk the perimeter of the park established from an old quarry in 1864. It is an oasis built from rock, high above the rooftops of Paris. I circle the park for quite some time and peer through the tall metal fence to see a mini jungle of unkempt trees and vines and large stalks of flowers and a profusion of plant life in its natural state. When I finally find a gate in the fence, I walk into an Alice in Wonderland venue. I rather expect to see Lewis Carroll's blue caterpillar sitting on one of the large leaves smoking his opium hookah.

Near the entrance is a puppet theatre. Every Sunday puppet theatres put on shows for children who come to the parks of Paris. Today the colorful doors to the stage are closed because summer is gone. I continue down the wide pathways. Joggers and skate boarders zip by as they enjoy the cool sunny day as I do. Over the hills and off the beaten path are smaller pathways, which lead to rocks, little houses, bridges and various nooks and crannies. So many places for children to run and explore. A lake formed from the excavated craters of the quarry is in the middle and a rope bridge crosses it to the Lover's tower high on the Hill. Not as dangerous as Indiana Jones, it creates a movie set, nonetheless.

I join the summer walkers and head for the Tower. From there I can see the white dome of Sacre Coeur and the tall, elegant buildings which surround the park on all sides.

This is a livable part of Paris where neighbors come to this green oasis to breathe in the country air. The park is not pretentious; people actually sit on the grass, ride their bikes, and jog wherever there is earth. No 'Do not walk . Do not sit on grass signs' exist. This is a natural spot where you can look inward and appreciate what is good about life – sunshine, laughter, light, and love. It is to be in the moment of openness and calm.

As I walk, I see a pavilion on a rising hill. It looks like a summer place, the kind that should be sitting on a lake and serving hamburgers, hot dogs, potato salad, and French fries, but this is France, so the food is a different fare. Inside white table clothes with pink napkins and vases of white and pink roses adorn each table. The clientele is not the bathing suit and flip flop crowd.

I choose to sit outside and enjoy the view including the parade of carriages pushed by proud parents and couples, old and young, walking hand in hand as children laugh and run up the paths.

A waiter promptly comes out.

"Madame" he says as he hands me a menu. I glance at it and realize that it's Sunday bunch. Perfect food for another perfect day.

"May I recommend this" he points to one section of the menu as he pours water into a crystal glass.

"Oui, merci" I agree since it looks delicious, and I am 'faim comme un loup" hungry as a wolf not as a bear in English.

A young woman is at the next table. "I come here often because it is peaceful yet full of activity.

"Do you live nearby?"

"Yes. I moved to Paris a few years ago and picked this area since it's not so full of tourists." Then she blushed , "Not you I mean."

I laugh. "I understand. It must be so intrusive. Every nationality in the world wants to see Paris. The stores, cafes, museums everything must be so crowded."

"Where are you from?"

"The United States - I'm hesitant to say that in these times of terrorists. It puts a target on my back. Ridiculous, but maybe the ugly American in the 1950's is better than today's image.

"I would like to visit your country and its many cities I have studied. I teach 'les ados', teenagers, at a college nearby and my students have a variety of opinions of the United States."

I do not comment on the lack of cohesion in my country. I feel we have been rocked to the core by 9/11 and still have not gotten up on our feet. The fear of terrorism is a permanent shadow. I zip up my jacket and tie my scarf tighter around my neck.

"It's getting cooler." She sips her coffee and I, my water. "You've been here awhile – non?'

"Yes," I remark. She is right. They have been serving people inside and those who have come after me.

"I will go in and get them moving. It is not acceptable. You always have to say something immediately. Don't assume they are busy working."

Fewer joggers run by, but two pugs pick up the pace and chase after a goose. This is a park to be enjoyed and not adorned with statues that watch you as you pass by. The sun still shines but not on my outside table anymore.

Soon the young woman returns and behind her my waiter with everything on a huge tray.

"Je 'regrette' the delay madame."

The young woman smirks. We all know he regrets nothing other than being caught being lazy and unprofessional. Presented in front of me is a perfectly poached egg in a porcelain bowl and a midsize plate with a salmon crepe and a generous scoop of sour cream. Another smaller plate is designed with orange and grapefruit slices on top a bed of assorted lettuce. A croissant, muffin and yogurt adorn yet another plate. My glass of red wine I sip and taste. Everything is delicious. "Merci mademoiselle," I thank the young woman not the waiter.

Day 26

OCTOBER 14

"The whole of life is about another change and while we are alive until the very end, there is always another change."

JEANNETTE WINTERSON AS QUOTED BY OPRAH.

I wake up these last days when it's still dark. My subconscious knows I do not have much time left in this city of my soul. On the high walls the ivy searches for the sun as it grows to the top. The apartments on the other side in another building have permanent curtains to block out the sun – mine are just lace for decoration only. I walk to the lace covered door and in the semi darkness there are lights on in half a dozen apartments. I wonder who lives there and what schedules make them get up so early. My years of 5:15 rising times are behind me. I do not need to get up, but my internal clock has been set for too many years.

Without a paying job, I feel I serve no purpose. I think of one of my favorite poems, *To be of Use*, by Marge Percy "like a seal bobbing black sleek heading beyond the waves "is an image she uses to show that one's use/job is important. I always felt like that seal diving into work – being industrious and self-efficient. Now I feel I must explain myself. Americans always lead with the question "What do you do?" Not what do you live for – what is your passion? "What do I do?" I should answer *I live*. I do the many things I wanted to do but never had the time to do. I do what I want, when I want. Most of the time I give no definitive answer. I should respond, "I'm a brain surgeon. I'm working at being 'Marie Curie' or 'Georgia O'Keefe'." Instead, my inner voice remains silent. Less is better – be a woman of mystery. Listen and let others think what they like.

I have enjoyed the routine of this place. I make my bed. Translation: I fold up the couch. The muscles in my arms have gotten a workout. I make my strong coffee and heat up my croissant, bread, or pain au chocolat. Then I take it outside and eat in my pj's with a sweater cast over my shoulders – rather retro chic. The worn metal round bistro table welcomes me to sip my strong coffee outside in the Paris air. When I leave to go home, the two red chairs and the table will be folded up to accompany all the other 'garden' things in the corner until another summer.

Today I am sleuthing like Nancy Drew of my childhood. I am going to a museum of police history in the 5th arrondissement of Paris. Located on the third floor in the Hôtel de police at 4, rue de la Montagne-Sainte-Geneviève, it houses artifacts and collections from the Police departments of Paris. Founded a hundred years ago, it shows the role of the police between 1667 and 1945 and displays objects, photos, and descriptions of executions, massacres, and poisonings. I read that disturbing occurrences by the police are not detailed. The cowardly acts by the police during the 1871 Commune uprising and more recently, the Nazi occupation in the Second World War are not documented.

I head out anyway. I hop on the metro to the Boulevard Saint Michel stop to see what they have. I am most interested in WWII and the resistance fighters that the French are proud of - not the despicable actions of the Police who did the work of the Nazis. That part of history is glossed over. I walk and walk to no avail. As I turn yet another corner, I find the building but discover that it has been closed since the summer. It will have to wait until another time. I decide to continue up to the Pantheon and sit on the steps in the sunlight. The day after tomorrow will be my last day, so today I'll see what unfolds in the special sunlight of Paris. It calls for a stroll through the Luxembourg garden and up to Montparnasse. Teachers and students are eating chips out of paper bags and sipping from bottles of soda or juice boxes. So much for French cuisine.

Such a luxury to be able to walk to the park and eat lunch. I'm heading for one of Hemingway's hangouts in the 1920's *Le Select,* a famous restaurant. In the 1920s, Americans flocked to Paris, where the cafes of Montparnasse served as the place to be. Unlike them I do not know where this famous café is. I meander through narrow streets and squares that become dingier and dirtier. I stop and there on a wall of a building located **at the intersection of Rue de Rennes and Boulevard du Montparnasse** is a barely legible sign. So small it could be overlooked and so dirty it is practically illegible, but there with blue letters on white is sign **Place du 18 Juin 1940** to commemorate the speech given by Charles de Gaulle from the BBC in London. He urged the French people to continue fighting for the liberation of France. I am amazed that right here was one of the spots where it began - the beginning of Paris' dark years of occupation. It seems all but forgotten. I wonder how many look up and see it. A body shop sign hangs overhead and traffic whizzes by. **This is where it began with De Gaulle's urgings to throw off the yolk of Nazi occupation. It had just begun, but now this uncomfortable past seems all but forgotten by these busy Parisians.** I wonder how many pass by, never look up or take the time to read. I find it sad.

Not too far away on the Boulevard Montparnasse is the restaurant/café Le Select. I order an omelet and a scotch for the American soldiers of WWII and the drinkers of Hemingway's group who came here. I go inside to use the toilettes and am rather disappointed. Remnants of the 1920's exist – newspapers affixed to the walls but it's rather like a shabby Italian restaurant. I try to image the characters in Hemingway's The Sun Also

Rises. Perhaps Lady Brett Ashley and Jake Barnes are sitting in the far corner.

I return to my table on the sidewalk and toast my scotch on the rocks to those of yesteryear when life seemed so direct and full of promise... when people knew where they stood in life and the road they needed to take. I sit and watch the people of today. An elegant older woman with short white hair passes by in a mid-calf draped gray skirt and a loose scooped neck tunic. She has beautiful skin and clear eyes. Old but not appearing elderly, she must have lived through the dark years of Paris. In contrast is a charming slip of a girl with short dark hair. Her long black coat is simple and unusually cut. She is unadorned – no jewelry no scarves– just the beauty of youth. The contrast of life. It's getting dark. I must turn back but it's too far to walk. Since I've been walking all day, I allow the metro to carry my weary feet to the Saint Paul metro stop.

It's dusk when I walk through le village de Saint Paul. This area has no crowds like the busy streets of Montmartre. The narrow cobblestone streets are nearly empty, and I meander in and out of the small green courtyards. The vintage, design and craft boutiques, antique shops, and art galleries are closing. The cafés are almost empty. A mist begins to permeate the darkening sky and I can almost hear the wheels of the carts carrying the nobility to the guillotine. The tall white buildings have windows, and the inhabitants can view the scenes below in the courtyards and the exterior ones on the streets which border this area in the Marais, between the rue Saint-Antoine and the Seine. At this turning hour of the evening, I feel the mystery of other times as I walk through the maze of cobbled courtyards.

Suspense hangs in the air.

A wrought iron bistro table beckons me, and I sit in a courtyard to order a cafe crème. The other white wrought iron tables and chairs are empty. It feels like the scene from Les Misérables – *"Empty chairs and empty tables."* I sip my black and white coffee in the company of ghosts from times gone by. The windows above the stores are lit and today's inhabitants have come home from work. Do they just accept their abodes like any other apartment, or do they feel its history and deem themselves lucky to have these unique spaces? The history is palpable.

Day 27

OCTOBER 15

"Be not inhospitable to strangers lest they be angels in disguise."

OVER A DOORWAY IN SHAKESPEARE AND
COMPANY BOOKSTORE.

This is my last day in Paris, so I am walking to a few of my favorite places. First stop is Shakespeare and Company, the most famous independent bookstore in the world; it faces the Seine. I walk through the streets of the Latin Quarter just as the doors are opening. I grab a table facing Notre Dame on the Île de la Cité. On the near side is the store's weather – beaten rustic entrance. The windows face the street, separated by a tiny pedestrian type island of a sidewalk. Entering the store is going back to the times when George Whitman established the store in 1951. He bought the name of the shop and most of its inventory from Sylvia Beach the original owner who established the original bookstore in another location in 1919 after World War l. She closed it as the Germans were invading Paris. George bought it years later and owned it for decades. He died a few years ago and passed it on to this daughter Sylvia, named after the original owner. History permeates the building and the sidewalk views around it.

The young clerks open the aged yellow book stalls in front. It is the signal that business as usual will begin as it has for decades. People still flock here. They are the ones who love the feel and scent of books not the packaged versions that arrive from Amazon with no personality or history. I will buy a book today because each one is stamped with a circle and the logo for Shakespeare and Company. The attraction of course is a that this was the first English speaking bookstore which carried books in English in Paris. When people felt homesick, they came here to be surrounded by their native language.

There is a coffee shop now attached to the side of the building again practically extended to the edge of the side street. I go inside and order a coffee crème and sit to enjoy the early morning view of Pairs. Street sweepers are cleaning the sidewalks of nearby cafes as the bells of Notre Dame ring. It is so glorious. I breathe in the Paris air for my last full day in this city that I love so much.

Sitting for two hours over a cup of coffee is not unusual in this city. Today no stranger – 'no angel in disguise sits with me just a black and white tabby beneath the table looking for crumbs. – I put my large white coffee cup on the ground so she can drink the last drops of my coffee with cream. She purrs and rubs against my leg. Maybe she lives in the store and was one of George's cats - like the cats that live in Hemingway's house on Key West or Monet's in Giverny. How many now I do not know – perhaps concern for people's allergies and for those who always carry disinfectant have eliminated the homes for these legendary cats.

I pick up my cup and carry it inside. There is no dishwasher, just 'dishwashers' and their sinks of soapy hot water - good enough. I don't' feel too guilty as I walk inside an adjacent door. The books in this part are first editions. I look, but I "don't touch". The price tags are too steep. I walk through the antiquated main door and begin wandering through the narrow corridors with less expensive books. From floor to ceiling they stretch and soon I locate my purchase. A first edition half in English half in French about the TV show Colombo, copyright 1968. I'm sure few people are invested in such a book; it was buried in the back with other mysteries, but I have a friend who watches this old series with her mother who is now George's age. It seems serendipitous.

Carrying the book wrapped in brown paper and string, I cross the street and over the bridge by Quai de l'Archeveche. In the shadow of Notre Dame, I walk over to the tip of Ile de la Cite to the Memorial des Martyres de la Deportation. I step down to the patch of green. The tabby does not follow me to this seemingly peaceful spot where I can view the Seine and both banks of the river at the same time.

The Memorial is dedicated to the more than 200,000 people who were deported from Vichy France to the Nazi concentration camps during World War 11. Then the government of France was complicit in rounding up the French Jewish people and sending then to the camps. This memorial does not just encompass the Jews who died but also political activists who were sent to die. Built in 1962, it is shaped like a ship's prow and designed so that you have to go underground to a crypt, accessible by two staircases, to view the bones, urns, literary messages, and 200,000 glass crystals which symbolize those who died. It is designed to make the visitor feel claustrophobic, which is true as I would rather run to escape this than walk through the tunnel to the bright light at the end.

Thankfully, I can leave. I walk into the sun and see a large golden retriever leisurely crossing the bridge Saint Louis to get to the other island. The sun bakes my back as I follow the dog's route to a livelier place. He goes to sniff under the tables at a café and I follow a narrow road – along the Quai d' Orleans by the Seine. I pass magnificent white apartment buildings that have large windows to view the Seine as the sun rises and sets. The road is not long. I dodge some bicyclists and continue as the quays change names until I am at the opposite tip of the Ile Saint Louis. It is by Pont du Sully. Few people walk onto this tiny space of free earth portioned with a few skinny trees. But it is quiet and speaks of a slower older Paris. A few benches are placed for those with weary feet or those who just want to paint the Seine or read a book in her presence.

La Place Louis-Aragon is a tiny tranquil oasis, a spot to let the world float by and to soak in the sun and think or not think about life. Dedicated to a French poet, born in 1897, this picturesque pedestrian park is dry and verdant now but there have been many springs when the winter rain floods the tributaries leading into the Seine and the tiny spot of land is covered by water. The banks that buffer the Seine are high, but in some years, they are not high enough. The winter of 1909- was one such winter. The Seine's water level rose eight meters more than normal and torrents of water churned up the river as debris floated by. By the end of January, the waters had invaded the metro, the sewage system, and all buildings' basements. People had to move around the city in boats and walk across makeshift bridges to get from one second story level of a building to another. Paris has seen nothing like that for a hundred years, but as I sit in this little park at the tip of Ile Saint Louis enjoying the beauty of the gentle flow of the river, I am glad I am here now and not then. I gaze over the river where the sky meets the river and wonder what it is like in the fall when the leaves begin to change and fall against stark starless skies.

The weather is warm, and people begin to stroll in with ice cream cones and sweaters wrapped around their waists. I get up and walk up the narrow street to the Saint Regis Café on the corner of Rue Saint Louis en Isle and Rue Jean du Bellay. I find tables in the sun with a river view as the natives walk precariously by on heels. Dressed in short chic skirts, dark leggings, and the customary black long sleeve sweater with a scurf wrapped strategically round the neck, they still somehow remain cool. The waitress is different. She has the same leggings but with a grey tight tank top, black skirt, black Audrey Hepburn flats and Jean Seberg short blond hair. She finishes her cigarette, flicks the butt into the street and asks me – "Vous desirez quoi?"

"Un expresso et un crêpe s'il vous plait"

« Chocolat ou fromage? »

'Fromage » I answer. It' is wonderful how great a cheese crepe tastes here – so different than a grilled cheese sandwich or a Quesadilla. It's the atmosphere – the tall, elegant apartment buildings, the breeze, the river view, the mélange of people walking by and the smell of the air – the smell of Paris.

I sat here for so long the air is becoming cool. People have untied their sweaters and put them on. The sun and the light is beginning to wane and the sound of 'La Vie en Rose" floats over the island. So, over the Bridge Saint Louis I walk. I pass the guitarist as he plays, and I drop a euro in his hat. He smiles. I wonder if he loves his street work and will have it as a memory in his old age.

By the time I get back to the flat, it is dark, and I must pack to go home tomorrow. My meanderings have ended for now.

"If you are lucky enough to have lived in Paris as a young man, then wherever you go for the rest of your life it stays with you for Paris is a moveable feast."

ERNEST HEMINGWAY

I am not young nor a man, but I was lucky enough to be here in these times in Paris in 2013.

EPILOGUE

Day 28

OCTOBER 16: I LEAVE

"All we ever have is this moment."

- D.L.DICKSON

Many moments have passed since my return to normal life. Life is change and I expect that, but the change and adaptation have been in vast quantities. What I have learned from my Paris meanderings is to appreciate the unexpected even if it's not what I want. My mother used to say the things you worry about never happen – it's the things life deals you unexpectantly that are the ringers. Amidst the unexpected I strove to regard daily life as a tourist with an appreciation of what might be new in my daily life. To be immersed in the common place of life: work, grocery shopping, errands, house cleaning, childcare and the extras of coffee breaks, happy hours, movie, or mall dates must be lived in the moment of doing. In these 'living moments' or 'moments of living' I need to fully notice what is going on and that is what makes the now unique. I must not think about yesterday and the activities of youth, for I am not the same person that I was then.

Paris taught me to live in the present. Paris air smelled different; her coffee was stronger, and her croissants tasted more buttery. I truly felt alive. Doing laundry and watching pigeons was the height of my day at times. Packed in my post Paris being, like the clothes in my suitcase, is the awareness that nothing is to be dismissed as too commonplace. The tasks, the moments, the tastes make up the fabric of our lives. We must live in the now and not in the dreams of tomorrow. In Paris, each day was a gift. That is how it should be here – back in the good old USA. Nor must I think about tomorrow and the scenario of ageism and the days when I will not be able to travel independently.

Since I have written this travel journal, some of the people I referenced have died: Helen Reddy has roared her last, Charles Aznavour will not be seeing 'Paris in the month of May', Azzedine Alaia's fashion creations will not walk down the runway, Anthony Bourdain will no longer travel and eat exotic cuisine, Judy Collins will not 'Turn, Turn Turn', - to every season. All have come to their final season and so has the Queen of Soul, Aretha Franklin, her anthem R.E.S.P.E.C.T must become our rallying song. To respect and cherish one another, ourselves, and our time here. It is not that I am completely aware of my daily minutes, hours, days but I try to bring myself back to whatever I am doing and think about that rather than the random thoughts that are in my head.

Life is so fragile and unexpected. In January of 2015, a year and a half after I left Paris two men forced their way into the offices of the French satirical newspaper Charlie Hebdo. The offices were two streets over from where I rented my apartment in 2013 – basically the street behind the laundromat. 12 people lost their lives and 11 were injured.

Later on, that year in November 130 were killed by suicide bombers in Le Stade where a soccer game was being held and in cafes and restaurants in other areas of Paris. My bakery class with Didier was in the stadium neighborhood. We expect the mundane not the tragic.

If life is not so exciting and rather boring, I can live with that. I learned that in Paris and afterwards. I learned so much about myself. I could navigate the city almost like a native. I had a familiarity and comfort level in spots that became my favorites. I enjoyed making simple meals just for myself and discovering calmness in my soul. I made choices without a lot of deliberation and 'went with the flow'. At times I was lonely, but I learned to use my time for growing into this different person I was becoming – more attuned to listening to my needs, more adventurous and more open to people. I am not an extrovert. Actually, more of an introvert, I was never the life of the party, nor did I want to be the center of attention, I try to regard each day as a gift and see how it unfolds – to expect the best.

As I walked the streets of most of the arrondissements, I made mental notes of which areas I would like to live in next time. I also realized that I would like a more structured stay. A course, a learning experience with other people, I feel that could be the best of both worlds. I again think of Julia Childs and how she was living in Paris with her husband, a civil servant in the US government. He had a purpose. She did not. She tried hat making and French lessons. Both were dismal failures. Her husband Paul Childs was so supportive of her.

"Julia, what is it that you like to do? "

"Eat," she answered.

"And you do that so well, my dear."

With that epiphany she began her cooking adventures. Julia was in the right time, the right place, and with synchronicity by her side she made the right decision. My interests are not in cooking. In fact, truth be told I could live on take out or better yet have a personal chef. The classes I would like to take would involve writing, art, or learning more French. So that is my goal to investigate what is offered in Paris, for whom and for how much. So, I not only did that but went on my second meandering trip in 2017. So that is the book that follows…– pre pandemic. I am so happy I went. My alone stays and self-reliance skills help me in quarantining solo during 2020. When the world is finally vaccinated and I feel safe, I look forward to returning again to Paris and incorporating the South of France in my stay. Who knows? Maybe I'll take a cooking class in Avignon, Sete, or Arles. I'll find one given in French and kill two birds with one stone.

Until the next time dear readers …. Dear Wallace awaits but cannot meander with you in London and catch a glimpse of Queen Elizabeth 11 for her extraordinary life is over. Make the most of yours… meander where you wish. Have courage.

The Seine flows as it has for centuries.

A BIENTOT, WALLACE* (DIANE)

*Why Wallace? As a young teenager I thought the name had strength and mystery. My older sister and I would take the train —our Orient Express - into New York City and pretend to be English or Irish. This was the beginning of my meanderings. We'd go in and out of stores, coffee shops, down streets and finally enter Horn & Hardart's on 42nd Street before taking the train home to Connecticut. It gave us a sense of independence.

Wallace was the persona I took on to armor myself for the adult world I would be stepping into. I thought it was an old sounding name. A name of a man or a woman. I thought of a woodworker or man who built buildings – a man who earned a living through a practical skill set.– a man of his word.- a man with integrity and generosity of spirit –

Then of course, there was Wallis Simpson. I knew she was America and was basically infamous. I did not admire her. I knew little about her, but that she cut her own path in life, though not a woman of integrity. However, she lived with conviction and just outside of Paris.

When I was uncertain, I would say "What would my Wallace do?" and try not to be afraid. My co-conspirator, Marcy, my next-door neighbor, and I would have meanderings in the woods and fields of suburbia. We'd build forts, make fires, explore empty houses, and plan adventures.

As my Wallace grew up, I began to shed that protective coat, but kept the English accent, the integrity of character, and the wish for adventures. To this day friends tell me secrets or concerns, often followed by a "Do not tell anyone."

Come share my meanderings, advice, and youthful dreams….

And I will keep your secrets - Wallace

Made in the USA
Columbia, SC
20 July 2023

Dear Wallace

They say age considers, youth ventures, yet just because we grow up, we should not stop dreaming. In reality, we have just forgotten where we put our dreams: in our son's baseball bag, our daughter's swim locker, behind our mother's chair, or in our file cabinet under 'tomorrow'/ 'someday'. Take a leap of faith, pull up anchors and pack your bags . Paris is always a good idea.

When I decided to go, I had no compass. I headed out with no provisions, nets, or goals. In childhood we are told to follow our dreams, but when those dreams have been met – what then?

We change. We no longer hear the drops of rain on rooftops and windowpanes, see the rays of sunlight that dance across the floor or notice the first crocuses peeking through the snow. Life's enchanting song becomes replaced by rigidity, necessity, even apathy. Age and responsibilities erode our 'joie de vivre'.

I decided to step aside and go back in time – a time with no great expectations and schedules. On the pathway to new dreams, I intended to fill the 'now' time of my own inner clock with joyous pieces of moments like slivers of chocolate and bubbles of champagne.

Put on your walking shoes and discover the streets, the sidewalks of Paris - her neighborhoods and niches, her people, parks, and pastimes, her cafes and corners and most of all discover yourself. Come with me. Be a single solo traveler and learn from my daily excursions the uniqueness of being yourself – courageous, adventurous, and living in the present.

ISBN 9798374598896

9 798374 598896

9000